THE
FAMILY
CREATIVE
WORK
SHOP

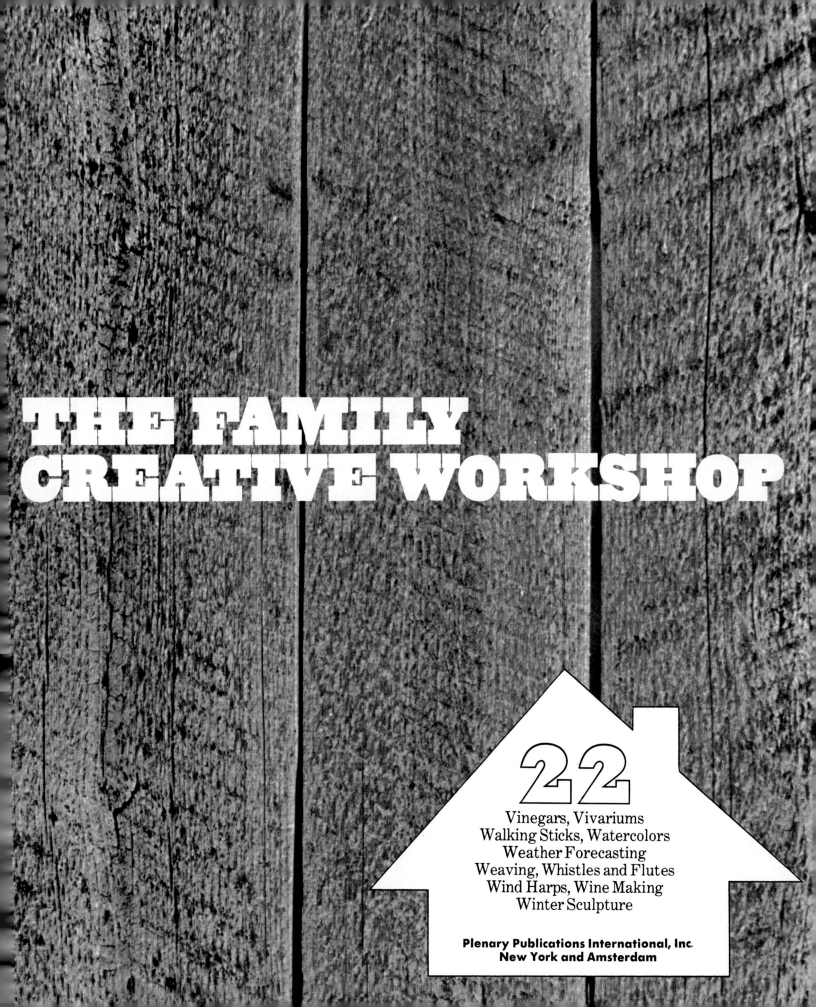

THE FAMILY CREATIVE WORKSHOP

22

Vinegars, Vivariums
Walking Sticks, Watercolors
Weather Forecasting
Weaving, Whistles and Flutes
Wind Harps, Wine Making
Winter Sculpture

Plenary Publications International, Inc.
New York and Amsterdam

Published by Plenary Publications
International Incorporated
300 East 40th Street, New York,
New York 10016, for the
Blue Mountain Crafts Council.

Library of Congress Catalog Card
Number: 73-89331.
Complete set International Standard
Book Number: 0-88459-021-6.
Volume 22 International Standard
Book Number: 0-88459-022-4

Manufactured in the United States
of America. Printed and
bound by the W. A. Krueger
Company, Brookfield, Wisconsin.

Printing preparation
by Lanman Lithoplate Company.

Publishers:
Plenary Publications
International, Incorporated
300 East 40th Street
New York, New York 10016

Steven R. Schepp
EDITOR-IN-CHIEF

Jerry Curcio
PRODUCTION MANAGER

Jo Springer
VOLUME EDITOR

Joanne Delaney
Ellen Foley
EDITORIAL ASSISTANTS

Editorial preparation:
Tree Communications, Inc.
250 Park Avenue South
New York, New York 10003

Rodney Friedman
EDITORIAL DIRECTOR

Ronald Gross
DESIGN DIRECTOR

Paul Levin
DIRECTOR OF PHOTOGRAPHY

Donal Dinwiddie
CONSULTING EDITOR

Jill Munves
TEXT EDITOR

Sonja Douglas
ART DIRECTOR

Rochelle Lapidus
DESIGNER

Lucille O'Brien
EDITORIAL PRODUCTION

Ruth Forst Michel
COPYREADER

Eva Gold
ADMINISTRATIVE MANAGER

Editors for this volume:
Andrea DiNoto
WHISTLES AND FLUTES

Donal Dinwiddie
WEATHER FORECASTING

Michael Donner
WIND HARPS
WINTER SCULPTURE

Linda Hetzer
WEAVING

Nancy Bruning Levine
VIVARIUMS

Marilyn Nierenberg
WATERCOLORS
WINE MAKING

Mary Grace Skurka
VINEGARS
WALKING STICKS

Originating editor of the series:
Allen Davenport Bragdon

Contributing editor:
Dennis Starin

Contributing illustrators:
Marina Givotovsky
Lynn Matus
Sally Shimizu

Contributing photographer:
Steven Mays

Production:
Thom Augusta
Christopher Jones
Patricia Lee
Leslie Strong
Gregory Wong

The Project-Evaluation Symbols appearing in the title heading at the beginning of each project have these meanings:

Range of approximate cost:

¢ Low: under $5 or free and found natural materials

$ Medium: about $10

$$ High: above $15

Estimated time to completion for an unskilled adult:

⊠ Hours

🕐 Days

Weeks

Suggested level of experience:

Child alone

Supervised child or family project

Unskilled adult

Specialized prior training

Tools and equipment:

Small hand tools

Large hand and household tools

Specialized or powered equipment

On the cover:
A lightweight plastic palette holds bright watercolor paints. With it are the flat and round brushes used by a watercolor artist. Watercolor painting is described on pages 2722 through 2733. Photograph by Steven Mays.

Contents and craftspeople for Volume 22:

Vinegars 2694
Modane Marchbanks, home economist.
PROJECTS: Wine vinegar; cider vinegar; flavored vinegars.

Vivariums 2704
Selma Graham, elementary school teacher.
PROJECTS: Guinea pigs; the English hooded rat; chameleon lizards; snakes.
Craftnotes: Making a vivarium cage for a rodent.

Walking Sticks 2714
Kenny Goodman, wood sculptor.
PROJECTS: Hiking stick; dapper spiral-design cane; sculptured walking stick.

Watercolors 2722
Fred Mitchell, painter and instructor.
PROJECTS: Creating a watercolor painting; stretching paper; washes; brush-strokes; glazes.

Weather Forecasting 2734
Donal Dinwiddie, editor and author.
PROJECTS: Making weather instruments; using weather instruments.
Craftnotes: Typical cloud forms and the weather they may foretell.

Weaving 2752
Bev Nerenberg, weaver.
PROJECTS: Plaid pillow; scarf with leno weave; twill pillow; twill jackets; weft-faced tote bag; wall hanging. *Craftnotes:* The four-harness loom; pattern drafts.

Whistles and Flutes 2774
Garett Alden, flute maker; Ursula E. Goebel, craft instructor.
PROJECTS: One-tone dowel whistle; a turned hardwood whistle; flutes; bamboo shepherd's flute.

Wind Harps 2784
Paul Dixon, harpsichord maker and woodworker.
PROJECTS: A simplified wind harp; a true Aeolian harp.

Wine Making 2794
Richard and Tom Walters, proprietors of Wine Hobby, U.S.A., Inc.;
Nily Rudner, wine hobbyist and instructor.
PROJECTS: Wine-making instructions; recipes for wines from fruits, berries, flowers, vegetables, herbs, and grains.

Winter Sculpture 2806
Jim Haskins, author, teacher, and winter sculptor.
PROJECTS: Snow sculptures; ice sculptures.

VINEGARS

More Than Salad Dressing

At the mention of vinegar, you probably think of a tangy dressing on a crisp tossed salad, or the preservative ingredient you use when pickling and canning foods, or perhaps a folk medicine. But if you had lived in colonial America or seventeenth-century England, you would not have considered vinegar fit to swallow. At that time, vinegar was used as an external disinfectant to ward off germs, to sweeten the air in a sickroom, to soothe a feverish brow, or to revive a lady from a faint. Gentlemen going for strolls in the cities, as well as doctors making house calls, carried walking sticks with flip-top compartments that contained vinegar-soaked sponges. If the foul odors around them became overwhelming, they would sniff the vinegar to clear their heads.

Today, vinegar is used mainly as a condiment for flavoring foods and as a food preservative. But some external uses do remain—it can be used as a hair rinse to promote shine, for example, and many herbal vinegars can be used to pleasantly scent bath water.

Modane Marchbanks of Englewood, New Jersey, is a free-lance home economist and a consultant to several major food companies. She is an expert on all types of foods— from sweet to sour—evidenced by the fact that she was the craftsperson for Syrups, *in Volume 19 of this series, as well as for this report on vinegars.*

Types of Vinegar
There are five types of vinegar for cooking and table use. Which one you choose will depend on the intended use and your personal taste.

Cider or apple vinegar is amber and has the smell of ripe apples. Its fruity taste helps to blend flavors. In canning, it is best used with dark fruits and vegetables, since it may cause darkening of light-colored or white ones. It can be made at home from apple cider.

Wine or grape vinegar can be red or pale golden yellow, depending on the grape used. This vinegar is not suitable for canning but is the ideal base for most herb-flavored vinegars. It is usually less acid than cider or distilled white vinegar. It can be made at home from homemade or purchased wine and can be substituted for cooking wines in most recipes.

Malt or beer vinegar is also known as British vinegar, since it is chiefly used in England, both at the table (sprinkled on fish and chips) and for pickling. It has a brownish color and smells like beer. Made from malted barley and oats, it is not easily produced at home.

Distilled white vinegar is a by-product of industrial distilling and cannot be made at home. This clear vinegar has a sharp, pungent taste and is used for canning when a light color is important.

Flavored vinegars are generally wine vinegars (although other types may be used) flavored with herbs, spices, or even flowers. These have a mellower taste than unflavored vinegars.

Making Vinegar at Home
To make vinegar at home, you add the bacterium *Acetobacter* (in the form of a starter) to a fermented liquid base (usually wine or cider). This bacterium converts the alcohol content of the liquid into acetic acid; it needs much air for proper growth and development. The quality of the vinegar depends on the age and flavor of its ingredients. Different vinegars can be blended, but this requires cautious experimentation. Vinegars should not be exposed to air, strong light, or severe cold; any of these can cause deterioration. If you make wine at home, never make the wine and the vinegar in the same room; vinegar bacteria could cause the wine to turn bad. For the same reason, use separate containers for wine vinegar and cider vinegar; never mix them.

Shown opposite are ingredients of the three types of vinegar that can be made at home: tart apples and apple cider (for cider vinegar); purchased red wine and white and red grapes (for wine vinegar); and pots of fresh basil and tarragon herbs (for flavoring purchased or prepared vinegars). Malt vinegar and distilled white vinegars are by-products of the brewing and distilling industries and would be difficult, if not impossible, to make at home. Still, either can be used, as well as cider or wine vinegar, as a base for a flavored vinegar seasoned with herbs, spices, or aromatic seed.

Wine vinegar

Any vinegar should be made in a small wooden barrel or keg with a bung hole in the top and a spigot on the side, a few inches up from the bottom (Figure A). If the barrel has no spigot, buy one and insert it.

Scrub the barrel clean and wait while it dries completely. Then warm enough good wine vinegar (4 to 6 percent acidity) to fill the barrel about three-quarters full. Let the vinegar stand in the barrel for 24 hours to season the wood. Draw off about two-thirds of the vinegar through the spigot and bottle it. This vinegar can be used immediately. The vinegar left in the barrel will be the starter for the next batch. Vinegar, like bread and yogurt, needs such a starter for each batch. Through the bung hole, pour unpasteurized wine in the same amount as the vinegar drawn off. The wine must be unpasteurized—most wine bottled in the United States is pasteurized; so check the label. Close the bung hole and keep the temperature at 70 to 75 degrees Fahrenheit for eight to ten days. This first batch of vinegar may be weak; it can be used when a more delicate flavor is desired.

The vinegar forms a thick film, called a mother, over the surface exposed to air inside the barrel. It is important that you disturb this film as little as possible. Draw off, through the spigot, as much vinegar as you like up to two-thirds of the total amount; leave the rest as a starter for the next batch.

Before you refill the barrel with wine, put a long, thin rubber, plastic, or metal tube through the bung hole and pierce the film covering the vinegar, but do not pierce more than once if you can avoid it. Wine poured through this tube will be forced to flow beneath the film. Use a funnel to pour the wine through the tube into the barrel; then repeat the aging and drawing off processes. By always leaving one-third of the vinegar in the barrel as a starter, you can continue making vinegar indefinitely in this way.

With Homemade Wine

If you make your own wine, you can make wine vinegar, too. Immediately after you siphon off the wine you plan to drink, transfer the leftover fermented solids to an empty vinegar-making barrel. Leave the bung hole open so air can reach these solids. When the smell of vinegar becomes apparent, fill the barrel to about one-tenth of its capacity with lukewarm water. Repeat this procedure with the same amount of water for seven days, or until the container is three-quarters full. Now open the spigot and draw off a little of the liquid at a time, pouring it back through a funnel and tube so it will flow beneath the film that should be forming. Do this once a day for a month to make a strong-flavored vinegar. Strain the vinegar through cheesecloth to remove the solids, squeezing out all the liquid, and bottle. Store the vinegar in a warm place and age for another month before using.

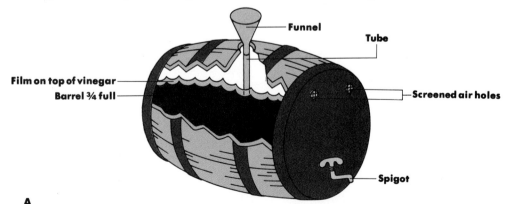

A

Figure A: Make wine vinegar in a small wooden barrel or keg with a bung hole on top and a spigot on one end near the bottom. Fill the barrel with wine through a funnel and tube inserted through the bung hole; draw out the vinegar from the spigot. A thick film will form over the surface of the liquid as it turns to vinegar. This should be disturbed as little as possible. Screened holes in one end allow air to reach the wine and hasten the fermentation process.

Vinegar pie, similar to a Southern specialty called chess pie, is delicate in both texture and flavor; the white wine vinegar and grated lemon peel add just a hint of tartness. The smooth, custardlike filling is cooked, then poured into a baked pie shell; no additional baking is necessary.

Vinegar Pie

Ingredients:

2 tablespoons white wine vinegar (cider or malt vinegar may also be used)
1 teaspoon grated peel from 1 lemon (a lime can also be used)
1 cup sugar
1 cup water
1 tablespoon cornstarch
2 tablespoons water
3 eggs, beaten
⅛ teaspoon salt
2 tablespoons butter or margarine
1 9-inch pie shell, baked

Place vinegar and lemon peel in a cup or small dish; let stand 2 to 3 hours until vinegar becomes lemon flavored (photograph 1). Place sugar, 1 cup water, and the vinegar and lemon peel mixture in a 2-quart saucepan. Cook over medium heat, stirring constantly, until sugar is dissolved and the mixture boils. Mix cornstarch and remaining water; stir into beaten eggs; add salt. Spoon about ½ cup hot vinegar mixture into egg mixture and stir well. Gradually stir egg mixture into remaining vinegar mixture in saucepan. Cook about 2 minutes or until mixture is thickened and smooth, gently stirring constantly. Add butter and stir in. Cool mixture about 5 minutes, then pour into baked pie shell. Let cool, then top with whipped cream or whipped topping.

1: The first step in making vinegar pie is to combine white wine vinegar with grated lemon peel, and let them stand for several hours to blend the flavors. Then proceed with the recipe at left.

Hot-pepper vinegar, made with chili or any other variety of hot pepper, can also be served with cooked turnip greens (above), kale, collard greens, mustard greens, or dandelion greens.

In many Southern homes, a cruet of cider vinegar flavored with hot peppers (such as the tabasco variety) is always on the table, ready to be liberally sprinkled over fresh greens. The vinegar can also be served over cooked greens (left).

Kitchen Favorites and Celebrations
Cider vinegar

The starter for sweet-cider vinegar is made of the peels and cores of a few tart, green apples. (These are comparable to the fermented-wine solids used as a starter for wine vinegar.) Cover the peelings and cores with lukewarm water, and let them stand for 24 hours in a warm place. Foam, the mother, will begin to form at the end of that time. Scoop off the foam, reserving the water for later, and gently pour the foam into a jug of sweet cider so the foam floats on top. In five to eight days, the cider will have turned to vinegar. At the end of that period, strain the water in which the peelings and cores have been soaking; this, too, will be vinegar, although of a different strength. The two vinegars may be blended or used separately.

To make hard-cider vinegar, add four tablespoons of whiskey and two of rye meal to each quart of hard cider. Mix well and let stand, covered, in a warm place, for three or four weeks. This vinegar will be stronger than the sweet-cider vinegar.

Hot-Pepper Vinegar

Ingredients:

¼ pound (approximately) green or red hot peppers (tabasco, chili, or other variety)
1 pint cider vinegar (malt or distilled white vinegar may also be used)

Rinse peppers to clean. Then drop whole peppers into boiling water; scald for about 1 minute. Rinse under cold running water to cool. Place peppers in vinegar cruet or bottle. Fill with vinegar; cap. Let stand several days before serving. Makes about 4 cruets for the table. Refrigerate extra if not to be used within 2 months. Serve over cooked or fresh mustard greens, collards, turnip greens, kale, or other greens.

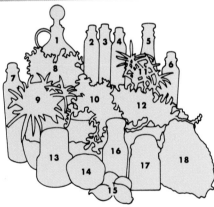

Flavored vinegars can be made with many different fresh or dried herbs, spices, or aromatic seed. Some possible ingredients, as keyed in the drawing at left, are: (1) cider vinegar, (2) coriander seed, (3) crushed red pepper, (4) celery seed, (5) red wine vinegar, (6) dried oregano, (7) curry powder, (8) fresh basil, (9) fresh tarragon, (10) fresh pineapple mint, (11) fresh rosemary, (12) fresh thyme, (13) dill seed, (14) garlic clove, (15) shallots, (16) fennel seed, (17) mustard seed, (18) a bunch of dried oregano.

2: To prepare a flavored vinegar, make an infusion by putting the vinegar base and fresh herb leaves or other seasonings in a glass container. Cover the container and set it on a sunny windowsill or other warm place for from 10 days to 2 weeks, shaking the bottle vigorously each day.

Kitchen Favorites and Celebrations
Flavored vinegars

Vinegars flavored with fresh or dried herbs, flowers, flower petals, aromatic seed, spices, or freshly grated roots add interest to the most ordinary foods. They lend themselves to experiments and are quite easy to make. An infusion is made by putting the base vinegar and the flavoring in a glass container and letting this stand in a warm place for 10 to 14 days. A sunny windowsill where fresh herbs grow is ideal (photograph 2). As the herbs or other flavorings steep in the vinegar, their essential oils are extracted.

Personal preference, as well as the planned use of the vinegar, will determine whether you use a wine, cider, or distilled vinegar as the base. White and red wine vinegars are most commonly used, but herbs will cause any vinegar to lose its sharp acidity and will produce a pleasant mellowness. The proportions of the base vinegar to flavorings and methods of infusion are given at right.

Basic proportions for flavored vinegars

Pour	Over
1 quart of the preferred vinegar (at room temperature or lukewarm)	2 cups of chopped fresh herbs
1 quart of the preferred vinegar (heated to lukewarm or boiling)	½ cup of dried herb leaves or 1 tablespoon of spices or bruised aromatic seed

3: If you use aromatic seed such as mustard seed to flavor a vinegar, bruise them slightly with a pestle in a mortar to release essential oils.

Seed tied in cheesecloth

B

Figure B: Instead of a mortar and pestle (photograph 3), a hammer can be used to bruise aromatic seed used for flavoring. Tie the seed in cheesecloth and put them on a worktable as you tap.

Flavored Vinegar Used as a Salad Dressing

Spicy Herb Vinegar

Ingredients:

1 teaspoon dried dill seed
10 black peppercorns
6 whole allspice
6 whole cloves
1 teaspoon dried sweet basil
1 teaspoon dried marjoram
1 teaspoon dried mint
½ teaspoon dried tarragon
¼ teaspoon crushed red pepper
3 bay leaves, broken
1 quart red wine vinegar (cider vinegar may also be used)

If possible, use fresh herbs instead of dried, since their flavorful essential oils are more abundant. To use dried herbs successfully, you must heat the vinegar before you pour it over the herbs. Aromatic seed should be bruised before you add the base vinegar; use a mortar and pestle (photograph 3) or a hammer (Figure B). You can blend seasonings as well as base vinegars, but be careful not to overpower a delicate flavor with one such as garlic or onion.

For the infusion, use a canning jar, wine carafe, large cruet, apothecary jar, peanut butter jar, pickle jar, or other glass container with a tight cover. (The container used for the infusion need not be the same as the one used for the finished vinegar.) Shake the vinegar once each day during the infusion process. Then, if a stronger flavor is desired, strain the vinegar, add new herbs, and continue the infusion.

Whether or not you should strain out the seasonings is largely a matter of personal preference. A vinegar flavored with a powdered spice needs to be carefully filtered through cheesecloth or filter paper. In other cases, since the flavoring properties of the seasonings are greatly diminished by the end of the infusion period, the only reason to leave them in is decorative.

A flavored vinegar can be used as a salad dressing in a vinegar-and-oil combination, be blended with mayonnaise for a creamy dressing, or be mixed with other ingredients. Vinegars made with mint, flower petals, or flowers such as lavender are especially delicious over fruit salads. Vinegars flavored with chili powder or curry add zing to fish and shellfish appetizers.

Pickled and canned foods are usually made with distilled white or cider vinegar. A flavored vinegar based on one of these can give a more subtle and longer-lasting flavor than the actual herb or seed, since it penetrates the food.

In cooking, flavored vinegars can impart their special seasoning to vegetable dishes, soups, and sauces. Or use them as the basting liquid for meat roasts and ham, and as the base for sweet-and-sour dishes.

Flavored vinegars also make excellent marinades for meat roasts, poultry, stewing meat, and raw vegetables.

Probably the widest use of vinegar is in combination with a salad oil as a dressing for a fresh vegetable salad. The spicy herb vinegar in the left cruet is a blend of ten seasonings with a red wine vinegar base. The recipe is at left.

Fennel-seed vinegar and oil make a pleasant, slightly anise-flavored dressing for a light lunch consisting of half an avocado stuffed with pink grapefruit sections and raw mushroom slices. Fennel fronds, delicate and fernlike, are an attractive garnish on the plate.

Celery seed mellowed the flavor of the cider vinegar used in the canning of this corn-and-pepper relish.

Crush dill seed, peppercorns, allspice, and cloves; mix them together with basil, marjoram, mint, tarragon, and red pepper. Place in glass container; then add bay leaves. Heat vinegar just to simmering; pour over herbs and spices. Let stand at room temperature 10 to 14 days, shaking once each day. Strain or filter. Bottle and cork, or cover tightly. Makes about 1 quart.

Fennel Seed Vinegar

Ingredients:

1 to 2 tablespoons fennel seed
1 pint white wine vinegar

Bruise seed, then place them in a glass container. Heat vinegar to simmering (almost boiling) and pour over seed. Cover; let stand at room temperature about 10 days, shaking once a day. Strain through cheesecloth or a fine strainer to remove seed. Bottle, cork or cover tightly, and store at room temperature. Makes about 1 pint.

Flavored Vinegar Used in Canning

Corn-and-Pepper Relish

Ingredients:

4 cups fresh corn (about 8 ears)
2 cups diced sweet pepper (use both red and green)
1 cup diced celery
1 medium onion, finely chopped (about ½ cup)
1½ cups celery seed vinegar (recipe follows)
⅔ cup sugar
1½ teaspoons salt
1½ teaspoons dry mustard
⅛ to ¼ teaspoon ground cayenne pepper

Remove husks and silk from corn. Place corn in a large kettle of rapidly boiling water; return water to boil and cook 4 minutes. Remove ears and cool under running water. With a sharp knife, remove whole kernels from cob. Place sweet pepper, celery, onion, and flavored vinegar in a large enamel or stainless steel pot. In a small bowl, stir together sugar, salt, dry mustard, and cayenne pepper. Gradually mix the dry ingredients with the vegetable and vinegar mixture. Bring to a boil over medium heat, stirring occasionally. Cook gently for 5 minutes. Add corn; return mixture to boil and boil 5 minutes. Fill clean, hot canning jars allowing ½ inch head space. Wipe top edge of jars with damp towel. Put on lids and screw on rings. Process in boiling water bath 15 minutes. Remove jars; cool on wire rack or folded towel. Label (include date) and store in cool dark place. Makes 6 half-pint jars.

Celery Seed Vinegar

Ingredients:

1 to 2 tablespoons celery seed
1 pint cider vinegar (distilled white vinegar may also be used)

Bruise seed, then place them in glass container. Heat vinegar to simmering (almost boiling) and pour over seed. Cover; let stand at room temperature about 10 days, shaking once a day. Strain through cheesecloth or a fine strainer to remove seed. Bottle, cork or cover tightly, and store at room temperature. Makes about 1 pint.

Pickled red beets take on added pungency when the vinegar used in the canning process is flavored with mustard seed and various spices.

White wine vinegar, flavored with caraway seed, and apple jelly are unusual ingredients in this red cabbage dish.

Sauerbraten is a special-occasion pot roast that requires advance planning. The meat marinade is made of two vinegars and spices.

Spiced Pickled Beets

Ingredients:

2 cups mustard-flavored vinegar (recipe follows)
⅓ to ½ cup sugar
½ teaspoon salt
2 sticks cinnamon (each about 2 inches long)
1 teaspoon whole allspice
1 teaspoon whole cloves
½ teaspoon celery seed
3 cups sliced fresh cooked or canned beets

Place flavored vinegar, preferred amount of sugar, and salt in a 3-quart saucepan. Tie cinnamon, allspice, cloves, and celery seed in a small square of cheesecloth, and drop into vinegar mixture. Bring mixture to a boil, then boil about 5 minutes. Remove spice bag. Fill clean, hot ½-pint canning jars with beets, allowing ½ inch head space. Pour hot spiced vinegar over the beets. Wipe top edge of jar with a damp towel. Put on lids and screw on bands. Process in boiling water bath 5 minutes. Cool jars on wire rack or folded towel. Label (include date) and store in a cool, dark place. Makes 4 half-pint jars.

Note: If beets are to be used within two or three weeks, canning is not necessary. Simply heat beets in hot spiced vinegar in saucepan. Then remove spice bag. Put beets and liquid in a container with a cover and refrigerate until used.

Mustard Seed Vinegar

Ingredients:

1 to 2 tablespoons mustard seed
1 pint distilled white vinegar (cider vinegar may also be used)

Bruise seed, then place them in glass container. Heat vinegar to simmering (almost boiling) and pour over seed. Cover; let stand at room temperature about 10 days, shaking once a day. Strain through cheesecloth or a fine strainer to remove seed, if desired. Bottle, cork or cover tightly, and store at room temperature. Makes about 1 pint.

Flavored Vinegar Used in Cooking
Caraway Red Cabbage

Ingredients:

1 firm head of red cabbage (about 3 pounds)
¼ cup butter or margarine
¼ cup water

¼ cup caraway-flavored vinegar (recipe follows)
¼ cup apple jelly
1 teaspoon salt

Rinse cabbage and drain well; shred. Melt butter in a heavy frying pan over medium heat. Add the cabbage and toss with a wooden spoon to coat the cabbage with butter. Add water and flavored vinegar. Cover and cook over low heat until cabbage is tender (about 10 to 15 minutes). Mix salt into jelly; stir into cabbage. Cook 5 minutes to blend flavors well. Makes 6 to 8 servings.

Note: Flavors are better if cabbage is prepared the day before and refrigerated, then reheated just before serving.

Caraway Seed Vinegar

Ingredients:

2 tablespoons caraway seed
1 pint cider or white wine vinegar

Crush or bruise seed, then place them in a jar or bottle. Heat vinegar to simmering; pour over caraway seed. Cover; let stand at room temperature 10 to 14 days. Shake jar or bottle once daily. If desired, strain or filter to remove seed. Makes about 1 pint.

Flavored Vinegar Used as a Marinade

Sauerbraten

Marinade Ingredients:

1 cup garlic-flavored red wine vinegar
1 cup red wine vinegar
1 cup water
1 medium onion, peeled and sliced
2 bay leaves, broken
1 lemon, seeded and sliced
1 teaspoon salt
½ teaspoon powdered cinnamon
½ teaspoon powdered cloves
¼ teaspoon freshly ground black pepper

Sauerbraten Ingredients:

*4 to 6 pounds beef (bottom round, top
    round, eye round, or preferred cut for
    pot roasting)*
2 tablespoons (approximately) flour
¼ cup corn or vegetable oil, divided
*2 medium onions, peeled and chopped
    (about 1 cup)*
1 to 2 ribs celery, chopped
1 carrot, scraped and sliced
1 medium potato, peeled and chopped
1½ cups reserved marinade
½ cup red wine
½ cup tomato juice
1 teaspoon ground ginger
Salt and pepper to taste
1 tablespoon cornstarch (if desired)

Place garlic vinegar, wine vinegar, water, onion, bay leaves, lemon, salt, cinnamon, cloves, and black pepper in a 2-quart saucepan. Bring marinade to boil; cool slightly. Place meat in an enamel or stainless steel pan; add marinade. Cover and refrigerate 4 to 5 days, turning meat once or twice daily. When ready to cook, remove beef. Strain and reserve marinade. Wipe meat dry with paper towels or cloth. Sprinkle with flour. Brown meat on all sides in about 2 tablespoons of the corn oil, using a heavy frying pan or skillet. In a separate frying pan, gently cook onion, carrot, celery, and potato in remaining oil about 5 minutes. Place vegetables in bottom of heavy casserole; then place meat on top of vegetables. Stir together the reserved marinade, wine, tomato juice, and ginger. Pour mixture into pan where vegetables were cooked. Heat, then pour over meat. Season to taste with salt and pepper. Cover tightly; roast at 300 degrees Fahrenheit, turning once or twice, for 3 to 3½ hours or until meat is tender when tested with a fork or tip of a knife. Remove meat; keep warm. Put sauce and vegetables through food mill or strainer. If thickening is desired, mix 1 tablespoon cornstarch with 2 tablespoons water and stir into boiling hot sauce; boil about 1 minute. Taste and adjust seasoning, if needed. Serve with boiled parsley potatoes, parsnips, and carrots or with dumplings or noodles. Makes 8 to 10 servings.

Garlic-Flavored Vinegar

Ingredients:

2 medium bulbs of garlic
2 teaspoons salt
*2 pints red wine vinegar (cider or malt
    vinegar may also be used)*

Separate bulbs into cloves; peel. Place garlic, salt, and vinegar in glass container. Cover and let stand in cool place 10 to 14 days. Shake or stir once each day. Strain vinegar through cheesecloth or strainer. Pour into bottles; cork or cover tightly. Makes 2 pints.

Marinated Bean Salad

Marinade Ingredients:

½ cup corn oil
*1 cup dill or dill seed vinegar (recipes
    follow)*
½ cup sugar
Salt to taste
Dash cayenne pepper to taste

Salad Ingredients:

1 16-oz. can green beans, drained
1 16-oz. can wax beans, drained
1 16-oz. can chick peas, rinsed and drained
*1 16-oz. can red kidney beans, rinsed and
    drained*
½ cup diced green pepper
½ cup thinly sliced sweet red pepper
Marinade (ingredients above)
1 rib celery, diced (about ½ cup)

Mix together corn oil, vinegar, sugar, salt, and cayenne pepper in a jar or bowl. Let stand about 1 hour to blend flavors. In a large glass, ceramic, or stainless steel bowl, mix green beans, waxed beans, chick peas, kidney beans, green and red pepper, and celery. Pour marinade over vegetable mixture, cover, and marinate several hours or overnight. To serve, drain marinade and reserve for later use. Garnish with fresh dill, pepper slices, and onion rings. Makes 8 to 12 servings.

Dill Flavored Vinegar (fresh dill)

Ingredients:

2 cups finely chopped fresh dill
*1 quart preferred vinegar (cider, distilled
    white, or white wine)*

Vinegar flavored with dill seed or fresh dill is the main ingredient in the marinade used for this colorful bean salad.

Chop dill, bruising gently. Place in glass container. Pour vinegar (at room temperature) over dill. Cover; let stand at room temperature about 10 days, shaking jar about once each day. Taste; if flavor is not strong enough, repeat infusion process with more fresh dill. Strain through several thicknesses of cheesecloth or a strainer. Bottle; cork or cover tightly, and store at room temperature. Makes about 1 quart.

Dill Flavored Vinegar (dill seed)

Ingredients:

1 tablespoon dry dill seed
*1 quart preferred vinegar (cider, distilled
    white, or white wine)*

Tie seed in a cheesecloth square. Using a mortar and pestle or a hammer, bruise seed. Place in 1-quart glass container. Heat selected vinegar to simmering (almost boiling) and pour over seed. Cover; let stand at room temperature about 10 days, shaking about once each day. Strain through cheesecloth or a fine strainer. Bottle, cork or cover tightly, and store at room temperature. Makes about 1 quart.

For related entries, see "Herbs," "Pickled and Canned Foods," and "Wine Making."

Selma Graham is a graduate of Southampton College, Long Island, where she studied early childhood education. She has organized several Head Start programs and teaches at the Eagle Drive Elementary School, Patchogue, New York. Her interest in children and nature has often focused on vivariums, including several designed for classroom use.

Animal watching has been a source of amusement and education since the days of the caveman. Early man learned to raise animals in captivity for protection, for transportation, and to see how animals live. Art, costume, music, and dance are all activities of mankind that were influenced by animal observation.

Today, few people are fortunate enough to live near a preserve where wild animals can be observed in their natural habitat. One alternative is the vivarium, a cage that simulates a natural environment. A home vivarium doesn't have to be elaborate to be successful. Its size and equipment depend on the needs of the animal being kept in it. A vivarium can be as simple as a wooden box, or the wire cage shown on page 2709, containing bedding (such as wood shavings or gravel), food, and water, or it can be an elaborate environment filled with living plants, a waterfall, and a variety of compatible animals.

Taking care of any pet that is completely dependent on you can be a rewarding experience. It leads to knowledge, responsibility, fun, and sometimes sadness. Children with pets experience the drama of life and death that is part of the natural world. Reptiles, for example, require live prey to hunt and eat; for some, a reptile vivarium seems cruel, but for others it is simply a chance to observe how various animal populations are kept in natural balance.

Choose the animal for your vivarium carefully. Although many animals can be successfully raised as pets, some require more care than others, or are expensive to buy and feed, or require special handling. The rodents, lizards, and snakes shown on these pages are good vivarium choices, but don't overlook such possibilities as turtles and frogs. Do not consider any animal that will grow too large for a home vivarium or any animal that is dangerous.

During the summer, frogs, toads, salamanders, turtles, and some snakes can be caught in swamps, woodlands, or gardens. But before trapping a wild animal, find out from your local conservation department if there are restrictions against keeping it, especially if it is an endangered species. If you prefer, you can buy vivarium pets at pet shops. Store-bought animals are usually free of the disease found among wild species and have become used to a certain amount of handling.

Rodents

Rodents are small mammals that have a single pair of chisel-shaped upper teeth for gnawing. They are warm blooded, furry, easy to care for, and often quite intelligent, so they make good pets for young children. Guinea pigs, hamsters, gerbils, and rats are all well suited for life in a home vivarium. Even wild rodents such as skunks (de-scented, of course) and flying squirrels are sometimes kept as pets. I don't recommend them. They are more likely to bite than other rodents and are most active at night. Many states prohibit keeping such wild animals in captivity. Mice are undesirable pets because they have no bladder control.

Reptiles

Reptiles are air-breathing vertebrates (animals with a spinal column) that move either by crawling or walking on very short legs. Among the reptiles are snakes, lizards, turtles, and alligators. They are cold-blooded animals; unlike mammals, they cannot maintain a constant body temperature. They can survive only if the air temperature does not drop below 60 degrees or go much above 80 degrees Fahrenheit. In summer, a reptile can withstand temperatures of 90 degrees or higher if it has water and a shaded resting place or cool burrowing hole.

A reptile vivarium should copy the animal's natural environment. Some come from tropical jungles, others from deserts. To re-create these habitats means you must regulate the temperature and humidity. In addition, the reptile must be

Mademoiselle d'Ary, a shapely Parisian actress from a bygone era, had her own charming way of handling stage props, here a 10-foot-long snake.

These children at a day-care center have made a pet of an English hooded rat. Directions for setting up a suitable vivarium for this type of small rodent are on page 2708.

Too large for a home vivarium, this boa constrictor is one of two that lives at Longwood High School in Middle Island, Long Island. Its native habitat of a South American jungle has been simulated with a waterfall, a variety of live tropical plants, and a pool stocked with carp and turtles.

The long-haired Peruvian guinea pig makes a winsome pet with a friendly disposition; it also has a hearty appetite, favoring fresh greens and guinea-pig food pellets.

These armadillo lizards have been provided with a warm and humid environment (between 75 and 85 degrees Fahrenheit). They will drink water from a small bowl, unusual for a lizard. They need a branch for climbing and a rock for sunning. Their diet consists of crickets and mealworms fed to them daily.

provided with live food. A snake will die of starvation if it cannot hunt. A lizard will devour great quantities of insects such as mosquitoes, beetles, and flies.

Only harmless, nonvenomous species of reptiles should be kept in a home vivarium. Poisonous species should be observed at a zoo, where they are kept under the supervision of professional herpetologists.

Environmental Projects
Guinea pigs

Guinea pigs are not related to the pig family, though they grunt and squeal; the adult female is called a sow, and the adult male, a boar. Native to Central and South America, guinea pigs are now raised as pets throughout the world. They have no tails, short legs, and a delightfully appealing disposition. They respond to attention and enjoy being picked up and fondled. Most guinea pigs are short haired, but there are long-haired varieties such as the white Peruvian guinea pig, shown opposite, which can be groomed with a pet comb like that used for kittens.

Guinea pigs are quite hardy and have an average life span of eight years. They are born with their eyes open and a full growth of hair. Some are able to eat solid food a few hours after birth, although most are nursed for three weeks. Start with a single guinea pig and get to know its habits before you acquire another, either a companion of the same sex or a mate. Watching birth is an exciting and rewarding experience for both children and adults. But be prepared to take care of the offspring or provide for their placement in a home or pet shop.

Setting Up the Cage
The size of the cage needed depends on the number of animals you plan to keep. A pair of guinea pigs needs an enclosure of about 1 square yard. Plastic cages are available in several sizes, or you can make your own (Craftnotes, page 2709). Commercial cages can be equipped with tunnels, exercise wheels, and connections to other units. With enough room, a guinea pig will usually use one area for sleeping, another for eating, a third for playing. Although a guinea pig likes to be picked up, you should not let it roam freely about the house. This will confuse and frighten it.

No special heating equipment is needed for the cage, although guinea pigs are sensitive to high heat. A room temperature of between 65 and 70 degrees Fahrenheit is best. Set the cage on a table or shelf out of drafts but not in a corner shut off from air circulation. Place two or three sheets of newspaper under the cage to catch food and water spills. Line the cage with bedding material such as sawdust, hay, or cedar shavings. I prefer cedar because I like its smell.

Food and Water
Keep food and water available at all times. Guinea pigs have sharp teeth and will nibble almost anything; equip the cage with a heavy crockery (not plastic) food dish and a water bottle with a stainless steel (not glass) tube. Water bottles for cages are available at pet shops.

Guinea pigs need vitamin C daily. You can provide this with washed raw greens such as carrot and celery tops, lettuce, cabbage, and other vegetables. In addition, feed a commercially packaged food in dry pellet form, available at pet shops. An occasional piece of fruit, a few nuts, or a carrot stick may be fed as a treat. Feed the guinea pig as much as it will eat, twice a day, but do not leave uneaten greens or fruit in the cage to spoil.

Cage Cleaning
To facilitate cage cleaning, keep a wastebasket or garbage pail lined with a plastic trash bag nearby. Change the bedding material at least twice a week, and wash the cage, food dish, and water bottle once a week. To do this, remove the guinea pig from the cage and put the shavings and old newspaper into the garbage pail. Line the cage with fresh bedding material and place clean newspapers under it. Wash the cage with a sponge dipped in warm soapy water. Do not use ammonia or other strong chemical that might injure your pet. To finish the job, wipe the cage with a sponge dipped in warm water without soap.

Breeding rodents
Most rodents are rapid breeders. Some, such as mice, are cannibalistic and may kill their young. Guinea-pig boars usually ignore their young. If you plan to breed rodents, find out at the pet shop how to tell male from female. This is not always easy, even for an expert. Guinea pigs are able to mate at about ten weeks of age. A female guinea pig can produce a litter in 62 to 74 days. The young mature rapidly and will soon produce their own offspring if left uncontrolled.

If your rodent escapes
Once a pet guinea pig, hamster, or rat is used to you, it will probably stay close by while you clean its cage. As a precaution, close all doors and windows in the vivarium room and have someone hold the pet. If you have a cat or dog, make sure it is kept out of the room.

Should your pet escape to another part of the house and be difficult to find, you can usually recapture it with a small trap designed to catch but not injure an animal. Bait the trap with a spoonful of peanut butter mixed with a little honey, sugar, or molasses. This will tempt most rodents out of a hiding place and into the trap.

Environmental Projects
The English hooded rat

Like many people, I had negative feelings about rats—until I observed a pair of beautifully marked English hooded rats in a neighbor's vivarium. My children showed no reluctance to take a baby rat into our home; it turned out to be a rewarding experience, one I have since shared with my students.

The English hooded rat (page 2705 and below) is intelligent, clean, and tolerant of handling. Its food costs little, and it can be kept in a small enclosure. All rats are prolific breeders; keep males and females in separate cages.

Setting Up the Cage

A 10-gallon glass or plastic aquarium tank is adequate for a single rat. Buy a tank fitted with a perforated lid and line it with 2 or 3 inches of bedding like that used for guinea pigs (page 2707). In addition, provide a hiding place where the rat can rest in privacy. Small evergreen boughs, cardboard toilet-tissue rolls, or 5-inch lengths of plastic pipe make good hiding places.

Food and Water

Attach a cage water bottle with a metal tube to one side of the tank, low enough so the rat can reach it by lifting its head. Put a small, heavy feeding dish in one corner of the cage. Dried rat pellets (sold in pet shops) provide a balanced diet, or you can make up your own menu with pieces of stale bread soaked in sour milk, small bits of celery, cheese, nuts, and dry cereal.

Although a rat is among the hardiest of all rodents, it can be injured if it is picked up by the tail. Lift and hold it around its belly. Clean the cage as described on page 2707.

This female English hooded rat takes time to nibble on a piece of cheese while she keeps a watchful eye on her litter of two-day-old young.

CRAFTNOTES: MAKING A VIVARIUM CAGE FOR A RODENT

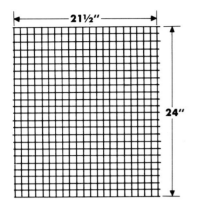

Using tin snips or wire clippers, cut a 21½-inch piece of hardware cloth (this is a screen of heavy wire and large mesh available at hardware and garden supply stores). A 24-inch width is ample for a one-animal cage (above).

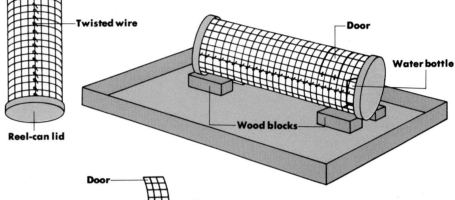

Fit each cylinder end inside the rim of a 7-inch metal can lid; those from some movie-reel cans are this size. Then lock the cut edges together by twisting the wires of the snipped-off edge around the other edge (left).

Twisted wire

Reel-can lid

Door · **Water bottle** · **Wood blocks**

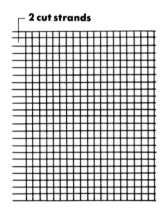

2 cut strands

Snip out two rows of crosswise strands at one cut edge of the hardware cloth (above).

Door

Use tin snips to cut a rectangular door measuring 3 by 4 inches. Cut only three sides of the door, leaving the fourth side attached (above). File the wire ends smooth. This door will be at the top of the cage, with the food dish directly below for easy filling. To close the door securely, bend it back down and twist one or two wires around the door and the cage.

Mount the cage lengthwise on a shallow box or shelf with a 3-inch rim (above). If the shelf fits against a wall, you can nail 3-inch wood strips around three sides. A cradle of wooden blocks or stones will keep the cage from rolling. Fill the box with a 2-inch layer of wood chips. Temporarily remove one of the lids and scatter additional wood chips on the bottom of the cage. Attach a water bottle inside the cage and set the food dish below the door. The animal should be moved in and out of the cage by removing one of the reel lids rather than through the door, used only for feeding.

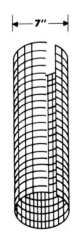

Roll the cloth so it forms a cylinder 7 inches in diameter (above).

If you wish, you can landscape the vivarium with an artificial tree or plant, twigs, and stones (below).

Environmental Projects
Chameleon lizards

There are many varieties of lizards in pet shops and in the wild. In nature, they are found on tropical trees, vines, and low plants.

Most lizards can move each eye independently of the other. A lizard will often remain motionless for an hour or more. Then suddenly it will catch its insect prey with a flick of its long, sticky tongue. Some lizards have lived in captivity for several years, but they rarely survive for more than a few months. They are delicate animals and should not be handled at all, even when the cage is being cleaned.

A chameleon (below) is a lizard that can change its skin color. This ability sometimes results in much teasing and stress. A chameleon does not change color to blend with its background; the color change is produced by variations in temperature, light, and the emotions of the chameleon itself.

If you put a chameleon in your vivarium, it will pose for you on a tree branch so you can examine it with a magnifying glass. It has five clawed toes on each foot, and can actually climb the glass wall of the cage. Few animals other than insects can perform this feat. Chameleons get along well in pairs, even in a small cage. The male is larger and looks more intimidating than the female, having ferocious-looking horns. It also has a dewlap, a folded neck fan that turns bright red when it is displayed to a female during courtship. The tail coils around itself like a spiraled seashell.

Old World chameleons are among the most intriguing of vivarium pets, changing color with changes in temperature, light, or emotional state.

The male Old-World chameleon is distinguished by his fierce-looking horns, but he attacks his insect prey with a long, sticky tongue.

Setting Up the Vivarium

The chameleon's natural environment is a tropical jungle with bushes to climb, branches to perch on, moist leaves to lick, and an abundance of insects to feed on. You can simulate this habitat in a glass tank about 2 feet square, covered with screen. Spread a thin layer of terrarium charcoal over the bottom; then add an inch of gravel or small pebbles. If you would like live plants, add a layer of potting soil mixed with sphagnum moss. Dampen the soil before you set in the plants. I use artificial plants with a few branches wedged into the gravel, plus a rock for sunbathing. These withstand the leaping of the chameleon better than live plants.

In the tropics, chameleons lick the drops of water that collect on leaves or rocks. In general, they will not take water from a dish. To provide water, mist the foliage every morning and night.

Chameleons must be kept at a temperature between 75 and 85 degrees Fahrenheit, and they require both sun and shade. Do not place the vivarium in direct summer sunlight or the chameleon might die of heat prostration. In winter, keep the vivarium near a heat source, and monitor both temperature and humidity several times a day. Dry winter heat requires more frequent misting. The proper light can also be maintained with a full-spectrum fluorescent tube placed inside the cage lid; a blue 25-watt incandescent bulb under the lid will help maintain the proper temperature.

You will have to become a hunter yourself to provide food for a chameleon. It favors small live crickets, but it also eats flies, mosquitoes, roaches, spiders, and beetles. A hard-shelled beetle presents a problem for the chameleon, but it usually manages to win the battle. Two or three insects dropped into the tank every other day provide adequate nourishment. In winter, you can buy crickets at a pet shop.

As with all vivariums, clean the cage and replace the bedding regularly (page 2707).

Environmental Projects
Snakes

This is a close-up view of the second boa constrictor that lives in a vivarium in a Long Island high school. The boa is nonvenemous; it squeezes its prey in its coiled body or holds it in its mouth until it is dead.

Only nonvenomous snakes should be kept in a home vivarium. Choose only species that will not become too large to handle. Small snakes like the garter reach their adult length of 1 or 2 feet in about three years and live about eight years. Medium-sized snakes like the king, grass, rat (page 2713), and indigo grow 4 or 5 feet long in less than four years and live 15 to 20 years. Large snakes like the boa constrictor (above and page 2706), python, and anaconda, not recommended for home vivariums, grow to 10 feet or larger in about ten years and live 35 years or more.

Depending on where you live, you may be able to capture a snake in the wild.

Although snakes have no ears, they were long the stock-in-trade of fakirs, believed capable of hypnotizing the venomous king cobra with flute music. In fact, the snake was following the movements of the fakir as it weaved back and forth.

Handling tips

All snakes will bite if they are frightened, but they readily adjust to proper handling. Snakes usually meet their prey head-on and strike from that position; so approach the snake from the side or back and pick it up just behind the head, never by the tail. Don't let its body dangle helplessly, as that would frighten it. Children should be taught to hold the snake securely, but not tightly. Let the snake coil around your arm for support (below). You can guide its movements by gently stroking it hand over hand. Regular handling gives the snake exercise and gets it used to your touch.

Garter and king snakes, for example, can be caught in many suburban gardens in late spring and summer and make excellent pets. But if you buy a snake from a pet shop, it probably will be fairly tame and accustomed to being handled.

Setting Up the Vivarium

The best enclosure for a 4- or 5-foot-long snake is a 10-gallon glass aquarium tank with a tight perforated lid. A 3-foot snake would have ample room in an enclosure 2 feet square. Since snakes are usually at least partly coiled, the tank size is not as important as the materials placed in it. A snake must be able to climb, hide, and bathe. The vivarium must be kept warm (65 to 70 degrees Fahrenheit), clean, and dry. In a damp tank, snakes smell bad and are also prone to disease.

To ready the tank, sprinkle a thin layer of aquarium charcoal over the bottom. The purpose of the charcoal is to keep the bedding material clean and odorless between tank cleanings. Cover the charcoal with an inch of sharp gravel, marble chips, or rough stones. If none of these materials is available free, buy a bag at a garden-supply store. Firmly wedge a piece of driftwood or a tree branch into the gravel so it runs lengthwise across the tank. It should have at least one vertical branch for the snake to climb. A rock or piece of slate, preferably with an overhanging ledge, is also a good accessory. This completes the landscaping. The snake will use these for hiding, molting, climbing, and sunbathing. It will also need a heavy water bowl in one corner of the tank. The bowl should be large enough so the snake can coil up in it; fill it with fresh water daily.

Keep a thermometer near the cage or clip one inside it. Monitor the cage temperature daily. If the temperature drops much below 65 degrees, the snake will become listless and will not eat. Unless the proper temperature is restored soon, the snake will die. Snakes also require some sunlight. You can place the tank near a sunny window for an hour or so every day. In summer, however, do not put the snake in direct sunlight. It will try to crawl under a rock if it gets too hot, but too much heat, like too much cold, will kill it.

You can avoid constant monitoring by installing a full-spectrum fluorescent tube (to provide the sunlight requirement) and a 25-watt incandescent bulb (to provide heat) in the tank lid. Many vivariums have outlets for these attached to the lid.

Your snake may be stronger than you think. For added security, place a brick or other heavy object on the lid to prevent the snake from lifting it and crawling out of the tank.

Molting and Growth

Snakes molt, shedding their skin as they grow. Young snakes in good health will molt four or five times a year until they reach maturity, less often after that. The cast-off skin will be replaced by a new layer.

You can tell when a snake is getting ready to molt by the change in its appearance. About one week before molting the eyes become dull and cloudy. The snake will probably coil up in the water bowl for a thorough soaking. This helps it to loosen the old skin. The skin may be shed in one piece, or it may come off in many pieces over a period of days. The rough surfaces of the gravel, rock, and branch will help rub off the old skin as the snake crawls over them. If the snake seems to have trouble in shedding the skin over its eyes or around the anus, you can help it by stroking the area with a small twig. Ordinarily, no help is required, and it is generally better not to disturb a snake that is molting.

Feeding

Snakes hunt and eat rodents and other small animals and are able to swallow prey much larger in diameter than the snake's mouth. The snake has an extremely elastic jaw which it can open very wide. All snakes have teeth to help work the food into the mouth, but only venomous snakes kill their prey by biting. Others hold the prey in their mouths or their coils until it is dead or unconscious.

Toads, lizards, mice, rats, and even other snakes are part of a snake's diet. Some snakes can be trained to accept dead food, such as bits of hamburger meat, but most eat only live food that they capture themselves. Garter snakes will eat earthworms and mealworms. Larger snakes, such as king and rat snakes, eat mice, rats, chicks, and hamsters. A snake will usually be satisfied with one mouse a week or a rat every two weeks. Large snakes can go without food for several weeks and sometimes months. You can determine how often a snake should be fed; if, after an hour, it shows no interest in its prey, remove the animal from the tank. A rat might grow bold enough to attack and possibly kill the snake. Never give a snake a mouse or rat that has been killed by poison; the poison will enter the snake's system and eventually kill it.

Clean the vivarium tank and the bedding materials regularly (page 2707).

For related entries, see "Ant Farms," "Birds and Birdhouses," "Insects," "Terrariums," and "Tropical Fish."

Mealworms

Mealworms are self-perpetuating insects. A quantity can be kept in a glass jar with air holes in the lid. Fill the jar two-thirds full of oatmeal and put in about one dozen mealworms. Add a few moist fruit peelings, such as apple or banana peel. Replace the peelings when they dry out. Mealworms appear dead during the metamorphosis process; they turn into beetles. The beetles in turn will mate, lay eggs, and produce another generation of mealworms.

Suggested reading

Encyclopedia of Reptiles and Amphibians T.F.H. Publications, Neptune City, N.J.

Gerbils and Other Small Pets by Dorothy E. Shuttlesworth. E.P. Dutton & Co., New York, N.Y.

Guinea Pigs and Other Laboratory Animals by Gloria R. Mosesson and Sheldon Scher. T.F.H. Publications, Neptune City, N.J.

A Pet Book for Boys and Girls by Alfred Morgan. Charles Scribner's Sons, New York, N.Y.

Pets by Frances N. Chrystie. Little, Brown & Co., Boston, Mass.

Snakes as Pets by Dr. Hobart M. Smith. T.H.F. Publications, Neptune City, N.J.

A Zoo in Your Room by Roger Caras. Harcourt Brace Jovanovich, Inc., New York, N.Y.

This red-tailed green rat snake is 5 feet long, but it has adjusted to life in a large pet-shop tank. The snake is a native of South America. It tolerates gentle handling.

WALKING STICKS
Something to Lean On

People have long been using walking sticks, but the popularity of these companions has risen and fallen over the years. Foot travelers have always used sturdy tree limbs to support themselves as they clambered over unfamiliar terrain, just as do modern hikers out on the trail. In addition, religious and community leaders in Europe, Asia, and Africa often carried large, ornate staffs as symbols of authority; these were sometimes carved with figures or symbols telling a story or delineating the powers of an office. In more recent centuries walking sticks from time to time have been fashionable accessories for well-dressed men. In America and Europe they conveyed status and sometimes served other purposes too. Some walking sticks had flip-top compartments to hold matches or other small necessities, others contained built-in pencils at the ready, still others were hollow to conceal a sword or a long, narrow liquor flask. A carved likeness of a dog, antlers as a trophy of the hunt, or an ornately chased and monogrammed silver cap were familiar decorative heads for a gentleman's walking stick. Even the functional umbrella, tightly furled, could be handled as a walking stick when it wasn't raining.

The walking sticks described here are not intended for medical uses; canes for orthopedic support should be fitted by a doctor. These sticks are simply decorative accessories to be swung, twirled, leaned upon, tucked under an arm, tapped, or used for gesturing as you add emphasis to the spoken word, Fred Astaire-style.

Kenny Goodman is a wood sculptor who specializes in carving walking sticks and large, Easter Island-type heads. Kenny had no formal art training; he began sculpting when he was an elementary school teacher and carved faces on bits of blackboard chalk. He also designs sculpted jewelry. His work, along with that of other artists, is displayed in his gallery and shop in New York.

Two ceremonial canes from Cameroun, a West African state, are completely covered with beading in bright, geometric patterns.

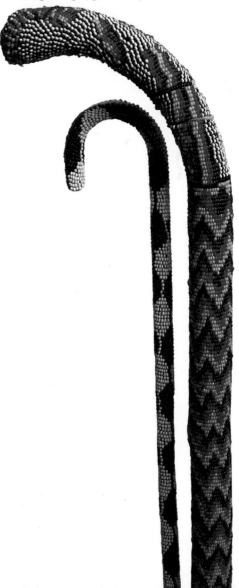

The female figure inset in the chief's staff (third from the right, opposite) carries her child on her back, Bantu fashion, and probably represents the chief's "number one" wife.

A back view of the ivory male and female figures atop the chief's staff (second from the right, opposite) shows the rich patina that is the result of many years of use.

The African staffs (opposite) are, left to right: a staff of authority from the Bambala people; a chief's staff from the Bakongo; a diviner's staff from the Bateke; a chief's staff from the Bakongo (see detail of the female figure, above left); a chief's staff from the Bakongo (see back view of the figures, above right); and a cult staff, used in initiation ceremonies, from the Balengola.

Materials and Tools

Wood has always been the main material used in making walking sticks, although some antique sticks are ivory or precious metal. There are two ways to make a walking stick. You can find a suitable tree branch, then shape, finish, and decorate it. Or you can buy a ready-made cane in a thrift shop to decorate any way you like.

The tools you need will vary depending on the hardness of the wood, the intricacy of your design, and your carving ability. Generally, a small assortment of wood rasps, files, woodworker's gouges, craft and pocket knives, a saw, and some sandpaper will do the job (photograph 1). Such tools can be purchased in hardware stores or at hobby or art supply stores.

The whorled head and spiral grooves of this hiking stick are just as nature made them. The carefully selected tree branch needed only to be cleaned and oiled to be ready for use. (In its natural state, it was the dark stick leaning against the tree in photograph 4).

1: To carve wooden walking sticks, you need a modest assortment of woodworking tools, including sandpaper and (left to right): files and rasps, gouges, a pocket-sized saw, and craft knives. Which tools you use will be dictated by the hardness of the wood and the complexity of the design.

Environmental Projects
Hiking stick

The rustic-looking walking stick, left, was made from a fallen tree branch of a pleasing shape and suitable length, cleaned and oiled to reveal the texture of the wood but otherwise unshaped and undecorated.

To find a stick, take a walk where deciduous (leaf-shedding) trees grow and look for fallen limbs. Do not take limbs off the trees, and ignore branches that are rotten or brittle. Compare the sticks you find for shape, and heft them to feel their weight (photograph 2). Try them for height and comfortable holding. When you find one you like, scrape away some of the bark with a pocket knife so you can check the color and hardness of the wood underneath (photograph 3). Tap the stick on the ground to feel for vibrations that indicate a crack in the wood, just as you check a baseball bat. A split branch, if otherwise strong, can usually be repaired. You may have to look several times or in different areas before you find a suitable stick; at other times you may find several (photograph 4).

You usually can repair a branch with a smooth, even crack (photograph 5). Use liquid white glue to join the two sections of the branch. Apply the glue; then wrap the stick with cord or heavy rubber bands to clamp the parts together. Let the

2: Study and heft the fallen branches you find in the woods as you compare their size, weight, shape, sturdiness, and markings.

3: Use a pocket knife to cut off some of the bark so you can check the color and hardness of the wood underneath.

4: On a single walk you may find several tree branches that are suitable for walking sticks, as well as others suggesting a variety of uses.

5: A clean, smooth split such as this can usually be repaired with white glue. Make such repairs before you clean and decorate the stick.

6: The first step in turning a branch into a walking stick is filing off the rough bark. A rasp with a handle is most comfortable to hold.

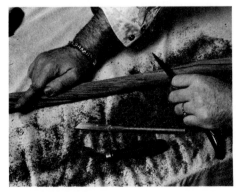

7: To clean the surface of the wood, scrape it with a sharp knife held vertically. Do not use water on the stick; it can cause warping.

8: After you scrape and sand the stick, protect it with a wood-penetrating oil. This finish will also bring out the warm, mellow color of the wood.

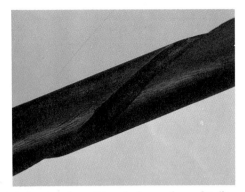

A close-up view of the spiral-carved cane details the simple but subtle design. The spiral groove was cut deeper in gradual stages, not all at once.

A handsome accessory for a well-dressed man is a slender cane decorated with a spiraling hand-carved groove. This cane, uncarved but with a silver band, was found in a thrift shop.

glue dry overnight; then test the joint. If the stick is now solid, proceed to clean the wood. Any repair should be made before cleaning and decorating to make the branch as strong as possible. If any glue has oozed out of the joint, it will be removed when the stick is scraped and sanded.

Start by removing the bark with a wood file or rasp; the kind with a handle is easiest to use (photograph 6, page 2717). Always apply pressure only as you push the rasp forward; the tool cuts only in that direction and dragging it back will dull the teeth. It is not necessary at this stage to follow the grain of the wood. You can butt one end of the stick against a wall to steady it so that both hands are free.

Next, scrape the surface of the exposed wood with a sharp pocket knife, craft knife, or straight razor, held vertically (photograph 7, page 2717). Take care not to cut into the wood. Scraping cleans the wood; water should not be used. Keep sharpening the knife—a dull blade can make you jerk your hand and let the blade slip so it mars the wood. Continue scraping until the wood feels fairly smooth. If you need to trim off the bottom end of the branch to make it square, cut it with a small saw.

Sanding, following the grain of the wood, will smooth any scratches left from the scraping. Use aluminum oxide sandpaper, starting with a coarse grade (No. 50) and graduating to fine (No. 220). Sand in one direction only, not back and forth, and change the paper as it becomes worn.

When all the scratches have been sanded out, brush a wood-penetrating oil on the stick (photograph 8, page 2717). The stick is now ready for use on your next hike through the woods.

Carving and Molding
Dapper spiral-design cane $ 🔲 🚶 ⚗

9: To establish the location of a spiral groove, wrap twine around the stick and mark the stick on both sides of the twine.

10: Use a V-shaped woodworker's gouge to cut a groove in hardwood. Start with a shallow groove the length of the stick.

The slender rosewood cane shown at left had only a narrow band of silver as decoration when it was found in a thrift shop. A spiral design was then carved into the shaft to give it an individual touch. The head of the cane was not carved.

You can decorate any walking stick or cane, regardless of its diameter or the variety of wood, with a design such as this. If the stick has been lacquered or varnished, sand it lightly. Then wrap a length of twine around the shaft and secure the ends with tape. Let your eye decide how closely spaced you want the curves to be, depending on the bulk of the stick. Using a felt-tipped marker or chalk, mark lines on the stick along either side of the twine (photograph 9); you will do the carving between these lines.

Remove the twine and lightly scratch a guide line between the marked lines with the point of a knife. Then use a small, V-shaped woodworker's gouge to carve the spiral, slowly following the guide line. Start with a shallow cut the length of the cane (photograph 10). Then go back and carve deeper if you like. Carving hardwood, such as rosewood, takes more time and patience than carving softwood such as pine. Continue carving until the spiral is as deep as you like and an even depth throughout.

Sand lightly to smooth the rough edges, and brush on wood-penetrating oil.

This shoulder-high staff cut from a tree branch has been given a noble sculptured head. The curved shape of the staff is natural; such an unusual branch is a find.

A gnarled knob of wood crowns a small sculptured head atop this walking stick.

Carving and Molding
Sculptured walking stick ¢ 🕐 🧍 🔬

Sometimes the stick you find or buy will suggest a certain type of carving, or you may have a favorite design motif you would like to use.

Before you make any cuts, draw an outline of the shape you plan to carve on the bare wood, using a soft lead pencil (photograph 11). Clamping the walking stick in a vise keeps it steady and frees both hands for work.

Start carving large areas first to establish a basic shape for the design; save the details for later. Work carefully, but do not hesitate as you cut; almost any mistake can be incorporated in the final decoration or sanded away. Use a narrow, V-shaped gouge to carve small, deep-set areas (photograph 12). A wider, round gouge works better in cutting larger planes, such as a forehead (photograph 13). With any gouge, make several successive shallow cuts instead of one deep one. This will reduce the number of mistakes, let you control the tool more accurately, and give you a chance to modify the design as you proceed. To create sharp edges, as alongside a nose, use the point of a craft knife (photograph 14). The long edge of the same knife can be used with a scraping motion when you want to remove only the surface of the wood (photograph 15). Do not try to eliminate minor scrape marks on the wood; you can sand them off later. As the carving progresses, the form you planned will emerge from the wood, and it may suggest additional carving (photographs 16 and 17).

When you are satisfied with the carving, sand rough edges lightly with fine sandpaper, being careful not to cut off the high areas you have created. Then sand the rest of the stick lightly, following the grain of the wood, to remove any scratches. You can leave the wood natural, adding only a coat of wood-penetrating oil for protection, or you can paint or stain some or all parts of the carving.

For related projects and entries, see "Carving" and "Sculpture."

11: Clamp the stick in a vise and draw your design on the wood with a soft pencil.

12: A narrow, V-shaped gouge is used to carve the deep-set recesses that will be the eyes of a face.

13: A wider round gouge is the proper tool for carving high-relief areas, such as the forehead.

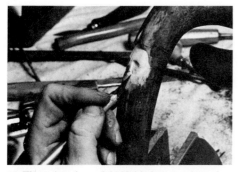

14: The point of a craft knife blade comes into play for making the sharp cuts that define the nose.

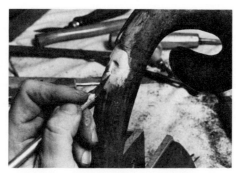

15: Used as a scraper, the long edge of the craft-knife blade cleans and smooths a small area.

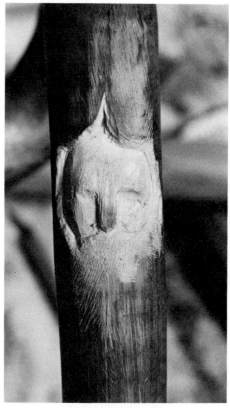

16: This is a view of the sculptured face that was planned, before any details were carved.

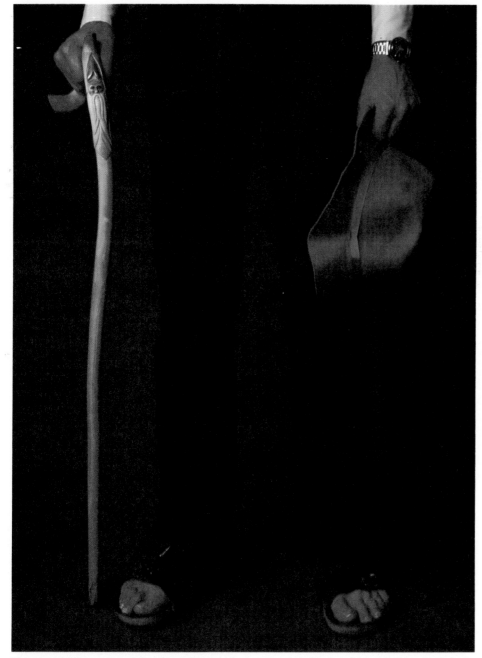

The wise old face sculptured on this walking stick gives it an individual, one-of-a-kind, handmade look. Gold metallic paint accentuates part of the carving.

17: The face had a look that suggested a long, trailing beard, so that was added to the design.

2721

WATERCOLORS
Rainbow Bright

The fingerpaints that are fun for a tot to play with and easy for Mom to clean up are an introduction to the world of watercolors. Then, with his first box of watercolor paints, the child can produce a rainbow of color. Sometimes adding too much water will dilute the paint into blobs that pool on the paper. From such accidents the child discovers that he can mix water with the paint to produce translucent images.

As the child develops an ability to coordinate hand and eye, he can begin to use a paintbrush to sketch with watercolors. Even then, the flowing watercolor will often take on shapes of its own. On the following pages are ways of treating watercolor paper and paint so you can control that union.

But the ability to handle watercolor materials is not all that is required in mastering watercolor technique. A child can sometimes create a beautiful watercolor by accident, but an adult needs a great deal of practice to produce the fresh, crisp images he seeks. A watercolorist must be relaxed, and he must be able to paint quickly when the inspiration strikes.

Compared with oil paints, watercolors are inexpensive and reusable. They dry quickly, enabling the artist to paint over one layer with another in a matter of minutes. Diluting watercolors into thin washes allows the whiteness of the paper to radiate through the paint, creating clear, brilliant colors in the finished painting.

Outdoor painters will appreciate that watercolors are very portable. With a minimum of supplies, you can move outdoors to make sketches or finished paintings. Artist Fred Mitchell made watercolor sketches (photograph 1, below) as he walked near New York harbor. Later, he used the sketches indoors as he created the paintings on pages 2732 and 2733.

Watercolor Materials

The advantage of painting in a studio, in addition to having all necessary materials readily available, is that you can paint during the day without being subject to weather changes, or you can paint at night. During winter months you can paint a scene viewed from a window, or you can paint a summer seascape based on sketches or memories. The basic watercolor materials for studio painting are shown in photograph 1.

Artist Fred Mitchell, a native of Meridian, Mississippi, studied painting at the Cranbrook Academy of Art in Bloomfield Hills, Michigan (where he received a master of fine arts degree) and the Accademia di Belle Arti in Rome. He has been a professor at the Contemporary Workshop in Art, Santa Fe; the University of Oregon; Queens College of C.U.N.Y., New York; Cornell University in Ithaca, New York; and New York University's Graduate School of Art Education summer program in Venice, Italy. Mr. Mitchell lives in southern Manhattan. His work is frequently exhibited in New York City and in galleries and museums throughout the country.

Opposite: Artist Fred Mitchell, working in the familiar surroundings of his studio, can draw his images from a variety of preliminary sketches. Sitting or standing before an easel are both accepted postures for watercolor painting.

1: In a studio, watercolor sketches made outdoors can be used for reference. Materials include a 16-by-20-inch block of prestretched paper; cellophane tape; flat red-sable paintbrushes; paper towels; tubes of watercolor paint; a plastic palette; and natural sponges.

Some artists work on several paintings simultaneously. The easiest way to do this is with several blocks of stretched paper bound on all edges; these are available in a range of sizes. The blocks can rest on an easel, a table, or even on your lap. A dull knife is used to remove finished paintings when they are dry. Other artists prefer to work on larger sized paintings by wetting a sheet of paper and stapling it to a board. If you want to work this way, buy a quire (25 sheets) of 140-pound hand-made, imported 100 percent rag watercolor paper. (Paper is designated by the weight of a ream, 500 sheets.) A convenient size sheet of paper is 22 by 30 inches. You also need: a staple gun; a large nylon sponge; a 5-ply plywood board slightly larger than the paper; polyurethane sealer; a nylon-bristle brush; and a cabinet handle.

Sometimes, stiff 300-pound paper is used because it does not require wetting or stretching. This paper comes 22-by-30 inches, but it can be cut into a variety of sizes.

For quick sketches, you need: a green coloring pencil that can be erased easily; a sandpaper pad for sharpening the pencil; a razor blade or craft knife; and a gum eraser. You can also sketch with a brush; of the many brushes designed for water-colors, the best are those made of red-sable hair. They are not inexpensive but they stay springy for a long time. To begin, get a round brush and a 1-inch-wide flat brush. You also should have a sky brush made of squirrel hair. To cover large areas with diluted color in even strokes, use a triangular natural sponge in a small size.

You need studio-sized tubes of watercolor paint, with emphasis on transparent colors. Select several of each primary color in increasing richness of hue, such as aureolin yellow, new gamboge yellow, and Indian yellow; alizarin crimson, light red, and vermilion red; manganese blue, cobalt blue, and French ultramarine. Phthalocyanine blue and green are two potent colors that produce beautiful trans-parencies when they are diluted. Add to these an assortment of earth colors such as a light olive green; yellow ocher (a mustard yellow); sepia (a sooty brown); and black. Include a tube of white paint so you can make translucent watercolors opaque. (When any water color is mixed with white, it becomes a gouache.)

For holding and mixing paint, get a light plastic palette divided into round cups and flat squares. The cups hold color and the squares are for thinning paint. Two glass or plastic containers, one for warm colors and the other for cool, are needed for the water you will use to thin paints and clean the brush with each change of color. Large fishbowls are ideal for this. Other materials needed are: transparent tape; paper towels; a storage box; plastic wrap; rags; and newspapers.

Outdoor Painting

For outdoor painting you will want to travel light. A collapsible, aluminum-framed folding stool with canvas side pockets is comfortable. The portable watercolor kit shown (photograph 2) includes a folding palette with a thumbhole grip. (On a cold day, you might also take a jug of hot coffee.) Before each trip, fill the folding palette with paint so you do not need to carry the paint tubes.

Stretching Paper

Stretching watercolor paper is a skill that calls for patience and practice. Pre-stretched paper in bound blocks is easier to use. But when you elect to stretch in-dividual sheets of wet paper, you will need to mount each on a nonporous surface such as 5-ply plywood, ½ inch thick, cut slightly larger than the paper. To keep the plywood from absorbing water, give it two coats of polyurethane varnish or shellac on each side. To make the board easy to carry, attach a cabinet handle to one edge.

If you are working with paper 11 by 14 inches or smaller, wet the paper in a lava-tory or laundry sink; a bathtub is more convenient for larger sheets. Hold the paper under cold running water until it is soaking wet. Then place the board on news-papers or plastic. Using a clean nylon sponge, wet the board and center the wet paper on it, making sure the watermark—a stamped impression—is on the surface side.

Dampen the sponge and squeeze some water onto the middle of the paper. Gently press the water into the paper, working it from the center to the outer edges (photograph 3). As you rub the paper you can eliminate any air bubbles that would keep the paper from becoming uniformly wet on both sides. You may need to sponge and press the paper several times before it lies flat.

3: Using newspapers to absorb spills, center a sheet of wet watercolor paper on a piece of ½-inch plywood waterproofed with polyurethane varnish. Press the paper with a damp sponge from the center toward the edges to eliminate air bubbles. Wet the paper until it is completely saturated.

4: Squeeze the sponge dry; then rub the sponge along each edge of the paper. Bear down with a firm, even pressure. This will flatten the edges and absorb any water on the board.

2: For outdoor painting, get a folding canvas stool with side pockets. Your portable watercolor kit should include a folding palette filled with watercolor paint; a block of prestretched paper; round and flat sable-hair brushes and a squirrel-hair brush; a capped jar filled with water; transparent tape; eraser; craft knife; sketching pencil; sandpaper sharpeners; and paper towels.

5: Fasten the edges of the wet paper to the board using a staple gun. Tack the midpoint of each edge, then the midpoints between them and each corner. Place staples ¼ inch in from the paper edge. Evenly space additional staples about an inch apart. As the paper dries, the staples will hold it taut, creating a smoothly stretched surface.

Once the paper is saturated, let it rest undisturbed for a few minutes while the water soaks in. If the paper gets soiled, reverse it and wet the other side. Finally, wring the sponge dry and rub the edges of the paper to blot up excess water (photograph 4). Mop up any runs with an old towel.

Use a stapling gun to place staples ¼ inch in from the midpoint of each edge; then tack between the midpoint and each corner (photograph 5). Space additional staples to keep it flat and taut.

Once the paper is stretched, you can paint immediately on the wet paper or wait until it has dried partially or completely. Your choice greatly affects the flow of paint. If you paint on wet paper, the color edges disperse into sunbursts that are difficult to control. By brushing thinned paint onto dry paper, you can make clearly defined shapes with hard edges. For preliminary sketching, always use dry paper. If you paint when the surface is mat dry, but not glossy, you can still take advantage of the reflective qualities of the white paper in your painting.

This sheet of watercolor paper was divided into four rectangles with clear tape. This enabled the artist, Fred Mitchell, to make compact sketches while riding a ferry in New York harbor. The quartet of studies depicts the base of the Statue of Liberty with the New Jersey shoreline in the background (top left); the twin towers of the World Trade Center and lower Manhattan (top right); the naval shipyard at Bayonne, New Jersey (bottom left); and the Statue of Liberty (bottom right).

When the paper is compatible with the type of painting you wish to do, place a strip of transparent tape along each edge (photograph 6). By masking the edges, you ensure an even white margin around the painting. This emphasizes the dual role of the paper as both a surface and color element. The white border also reserves space for signing and framing. On prestretched paper blocks, tape keeps color from seeping around the edges. Tape can also be used to divide paper into squares or rectangles so you can make several independent sketches on one sheet (above).

Sketching

Sometimes, before painting, it is helpful to establish a composition with a green sketch pencil. Sharpen the pencil with a craft knife; then rotate the tip on a sandpaper pad to make a sharp point. Sketch marks can be easily removed with a gum eraser once the painting is dry. Dust erasures away with a nylon brush.

Sketching with a brush is also good practice. To do this, use light colors such as manganese blue or aureolin yellow which can be easily painted over later with

6: Before painting, put a strip of transparent tape along each edge of the watercolor paper. Masking the edges creates an even white border to set off the finished picture.

7: For sketching with a brush, pick up mixed color from the palette and stroke the brush tip over a paper towel. This blots excess moisture so you can control the flow of color. With a round-tipped brush, gently rotate the tip to compress the brush hairs into a point. With a flat-tipped brush, lightly pass the flat edge over the toweling before applying the color.

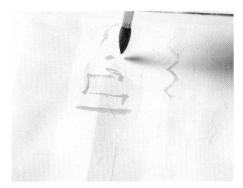

8: Use a round brush to draw with colors of different values over background washes (page 2728). As you gain the ability to control such brushstrokes, exaggerate the vertical and horizontal lines within the composition to determine the effects you can get.

As Mitchell ascended the old Capitoline Hill in Rome, he sketched with a brush to record his impressions of the ruins. The result was this painting, *Roman Journal*, depicting (from top to bottom row): masonry and foliage; forms projecting from cracks in walls; broken columns; and a fragment of a sculptured hand.

darker colors. Put a dab of paint into a square compartment of the palette by squeezing the tube from its bottom. Cap the tube immediately. Dip a round sable-hair brush into clean water. Then thin the paint with the brush until it is evenly mixed. To remove excess moisture before applying color to the paper, pass the brush over a paper towel (photograph 7). If the paint appears watery, add more paint to the palette. If it is pasty, rewet the brush and dilute the paint again. As you test the paint, bring the brush to a point. With a round-tipped brush, gently rotate the brush on the paper towel until a springy and precise point is made to guide the flow of the paint. When using a flat-tipped brush, wipe the brush across the paper towel before painting. With practice you will gain confidence in your ability to lay down sharp, clear lines with a purpose (photograph 8). In *Roman Journal* (above) sketched brushstrokes form the finished painting. As Fred Mitchell ascended a hill he painted the changing aspects of things with symbols that excited him.

Graded wash

Flat wash

A

Figure A: You can create shapes and shade objects with transparent washes of color like these. To apply a graded wash (top), tilt the paper downward. This lets water flow downward from the brush. Working from top to bottom, gradually decrease pressure on the brush so the paint, being more diluted, becomes lighter. A flat wash (bottom) is applied with a steady, even pressure on the brush, making a solid block of uniform color.

9: Begin to build the painting with washes graded from light to dark. Flat washes can be used, but they should be light in color. Use a flat brush to wash broad areas of color, a round-tipped brush for underlining and shading them.

Washes, Building Blocks of Color

Transparent thin areas of color called washes are a basic ingredient of watercolor painting. A graded wash displays tonal transitions from dark to light, while a flat wash is a smooth and evenly applied area of color. When you work with watercolors for the first time, practice making washes of several colors on a separate sheet of paper (photograph 9).

When you apply washes, start at the top of the paper and work down to the bottom to keep your painting arm from smearing the wet paint. Your free arm can rest on the edge of the paper to steady it and to guide your painting arm. Working from top to bottom allows you to paint in several areas of the paper while other areas are drying. Since watercolors dry quickly, thin the paint for several washes on the palette in advance; then mix other colors as you need them.

Watercolorists rely on the whiteness of the paper to supply light in the painting. When working outdoors, the way the light strikes objects and reflects from sky and water becomes an important element in the painting. When you paint an outdoor scene in an indoor studio, it is a good practice to begin with the lightest color washes, since these can underlie subsequent layers of paint. This lets the lightness of the paper radiate through the paint and creates a feeling of natural light in the finished painting.

For practice, make a graded wash with a yellow such as new gamboge and a flat wash with cobalt blue (Figure A). First, use a damp sponge to moisten the surface of the watercolor paper where the washes are to be applied. When the water is absorbed, your paint will flow easily, even if you use a delicate brushstroke.

To make a graded wash, tilt the paper to let paint flow downward as it leaves the brush. Draw the flat brush down the paper, pressing boldly at first and then gradually easing up. At the end of the stroke, gently lift the brush. The graded wash should become lighter in color from start to finish, as shown by the yellow square in Figure A. It takes a great deal of practice to make a graded wash that subtly changes tonal quality. But once you master the technique, you can use it to achieve a wide range of dramatic effects. Depending on what you are painting, you can use graded washes to shape objects, to give dimension to shapes, or to give the illusion of expanses of space. The latter use is illustrated in *The Last Voyage of the Queen Elizabeth* (opposite, top).

To make a flat wash, apply the paint with a bold, continuous stroke, bearing down on the brush with smooth, even pressure. The strokes should be a uniform color throughout, like the blue square at the bottom of Figure A. Flat washes have clearly defined edges. *Improvisation on Governors Island* (opposite, bottom) was made primarily with flat washes.

Graded washes, from dark to light, were used in this painting of the Queen Elizabeth as she embarked on her last voyage from New York harbor. The overlapping graded washes emphasize the boat's movement through the water and against the sky. The unpainted foreground appears vast.

This painting, *Improvisation on Governors Island*, was made almost entirely with flat washes of color. The elements of this composition—an old brick fort, puffs of smoke from a passing tugboat, and flowering summer trees—are interpreted with flat washes. The contrast of soft, flowing forms with hard-edged architectural shapes creates balance.

Dry-brush strokes were combined with the wet-paint technique to create the texture and movement in this painting of two cats at play, *Buddy Budds and Friend*. The pebbly surface of the watercolor paper shows in the white stripes of the cat at left and the tip of the cat's dry-brushed tail at right. Wet layers of transparent paint shade and soften the furry forms.

Dry-Brush Strokes

The brilliance of a watercolor painting depends on a balance of light and color. To let the white background shine through the finished painting, begin with graded washes of the lightest colors and gradually work toward flat washes of the darkest colors. On uncolored areas of the paper, you can take advantage of the pebbly surface of the paper to create grainy textural effects with dry-brush strokes. This technique is illustrated in the painting *Buddy Budds and Friend* (above).

To make dry-brush strokes, pick up a small amount of undiluted color on a dry brush. Pass the brush over a dry section of the paper. The combination of undiluted paint and dry paper will create an uneven layer of color as the paint is only transferred to the raised areas of the paper. Such dry-brush strokes are rich in color and texture; yet they let the white paper in the depressions of the paper show through in the finished painting.

Veils of Color

Since watercolors are transparent, you can create new colors simply by painting another color over a layer of dry or by mixing it into wet color. Demonstrated in photograph 10 is the effect of brushing a wet wash of cobalt blue into a wet yellow ground, a technique known as wet-into-wet. The blue washes suggest shadows at the sides and bottoms of objects. Glazing, a process of building layers of color to create new colors, is illustrated in Figure B with graded washes of three primary

10: By applying a stroke of blue over a still-wet yellow background, the artist creates a blue-green shadow line with a process know as glazing. This can be done when the painting surface is wet, as here, or when the paint is completely dry. For steady brushstrokes, press your free hand against an unpainted edge of the paper for leverage. Take a deep breath and hold it as you make the stroke.

B

Figure B: By glazing—passing one transparent watercolor over another—you can make new colors. At the top are graded washes of each of three primary colors, made with a flat brush. Below them are glazes made by overlapping the stripes with the same colors. Wherever two different primaries cross, a new secondary color is made. Red changes yellow to orange and blue to purple. Yellow turns red to a light red-orange, and blue is warmed to green. Blue converts red to deep purple and changes yellow to green.

Washes of wet paint glazed over a wet background were used to shade planets in this fantasy called *Laughing Astronauts*. In some areas, forms evolved from the way the paint flowed onto the paper. Starting with light washes of primary colors, the artist gradually created other colors with glazes—the process of painting one color over another.

11: Occasionally a small natural sponge is useful to remove excess paint from the paper. To do this, moisten a tip of the sponge, then squeeze it dry. Gently wipe the paint until you have removed as much color as you wish. Then clean the sponge.

colors. The wet-into-wet method was used to create secondary colors and to emphasize shapes in *Laughing Astronauts* (above).

Sometimes it is necessary to dry a wet area by removing wet watercolor. With a clean moist sponge, you can lift as much of the unwanted color as you wish (photograph 11). Clean the sponge each time that you remove color.

Freshness and spontaneity are important elements in watercolor painting. Artist Fred Mitchell was not pleased with the harbor painting above, based on the three harbor studies on page 2723. With a second effort, the artist painted the abstract harbor study opposite which pleased him more, although it was based on the same reference sketches.

Starting Over

Unlike an oil painting, you cannot "white" out the watercolor paper with fresh paint to reclaim the painting surface. When you are dissatisfied, stretch another piece of watercolor paper and start a new painting, as illustrated above and opposite. With each sketch your conception of the painting will change. Use these sketches to gather your thoughts. This will bring you closer to making the final painting.

Cleaning Up

Water is all you need to remove watercolor paints from art materials or clothes. But take special care of your brushes to guard their resiliency. Wash the brushes with lukewarm water; do not use hot water, as it may loosen the brush hairs and make metal binders corrode. Rub the brush tip over a bar of mild soap. Then gently press the brush hairs to work up a lather. Rinse the brush hairs under cold running water until all color is removed.

Let unused paint dry in the palette cups; then cover the palette with clear plastic wrap to prevent mildew or dust from contaminating the paint. To reuse the dry color, add several drops of water to the paint. Use the tip of a small, old paintbrush to gently stir the paint until it is ready to use again. If the paint is lumpy, it should be discarded.

Storing

When your finished watercolor is completely dry, remove the transparent tape from the paper by carefully peeling it back. Then use a staple remover to lift the staples. To remove a painting from a prestretched paper block, separate it from the

sheets underneath with a dull knife. Insert the knife in the slot centered along the front edge of the block. Slowly work the knife to the corners of the block; then gently lift the sides and back.

Use a pencil to title and sign the painting along its bottom edge. Store the painting in a large, shallow drawer or museum box to keep the paper clean and flat. Label the bin with the month and year in which the painting was completed.

Framing

When you frame a watercolor painting, do not apply ordinary glue, tape, or paper to the watercolor paper. Most adhesives and other papers tend to yellow the watercolor paper after a period of time. The only adhesive that is safe to use is wheat paste. And the only papers safe to use are 100-percent rag board, mulberry paper, or rice paper. For framing, select a 2- and a 4-ply 100-percent rag board the same size as the frame. With a ruler and pencil, mark an opening on the 4-ply board to leave a border as wide as you wish around the painting. Rest the board on a worktable and cut the opening with a straightedge and craft knife. Next position the watercolor face up on the 2-ply backing. Using a pencil, mark each corner of the painting on the backing. Remove the painting. Cut four ½-by-1½-inch strips of mulberry or rice paper. Fold each strip in half to make hinges. Mix wheat paste and brush it over an outer edge of each hinge. With the folded edge on top, position and fasten each hinge inside the marked corners. Then brush wheat paste on the top of each hinge. Position the watercolor on the hinges. Put a paper towel over each corner of the painting, and hold it in place with a small weight until the paste is dry. Finally, position the window over the painting and place the sandwich in the picture frame.

For related projects and entries, see "Calligraphy," "Framing," "Oil Painting," "Preschool Activities," "Stone Painting," and "Supergraphics."

WEATHER FORECASTING
What Will Tomorrow Bring?

Donal Dinwiddie, a former editor of Popular Mechanics magazine, has been a writer and editor of crafts and science articles for 19 years. He is also the author of a book on weather forecasting.

The man who said everybody talks about the weather but nobody does anything about it was mistaken. For centuries, people have been doing a lot about the weather—studying it closely and trying, with some success, to predict what it would do next and why.

Some early ideas about weather seem quaint today. One notion was that wise gods created rain to help man, but sent hail and lightning to chastise him for his evil ways. Another was that winds come from the exhaling earth and that only sulfurous winds could cause hurricanes. Still another was that raindrops are rounded because their corners are rubbed off when they collide.

The early weather watchers tried to find explanations for weather phenomena they could see or feel but had no instruments to measure. A great puzzle to them were the clouds that mysteriously form, change shape, and disappear. Since many clouds were close to earth (some even ringing the tops of mountains or, as fog, touching the earth), it was natural to think they came out of the earth. But that didn't explain how clouds, made of water heavier than air, could float. The answer, as it turned out, is that clouds don't float. Every particle in them, if left alone, would slowly sink. But rising air currents may push them upward. Or the bottom of the cloud may simply disappear as warm temperatures near the earth dissolve the sinking droplets of moisture.

Early observers did note the kind of local weather changes you may experience. If you live within 30 miles of a large body of water, for example, on a sunny day you can expect a breeze from the water starting about midmorning and lasting until evening (Figure A). The sun heats land faster than water, and air above the land expands and rises. It is replaced by heavier, cooler air moving in from the water as a sea breeze. (All winds or breezes are named for the direction from which they come.) At night, land cools more rapidly than water, air over the land becomes heavier than air over the water, and the flow of air is reversed, creating a land breeze (Figure B).

In the same way, daytime heating of the floor and slopes of a valley can create a slow movement of air (a valley breeze) up the mountainside (Figure C). And rapid nighttime cooling of a mountain slope sends cooler, denser air (a mountain breeze) down into the valley (Figure D). If a sea breeze combines with a valley breeze, or a land breeze with a mountain breeze, strong winds may occur. But they are rarely as strong as those that accompany storms. Early weather watchers were puzzled by where the big storms came from.

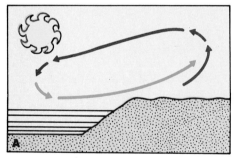

Figure A: On a sunny day, a sea breeze occurs when air over land heats quickly, expands, and rises, to be replaced by cooler, heavier air moving in from over the water.

Figure B: At night, a land breeze occurs when air over land cools quickly, becomes heavier, and flows out to replace the warmer, lighter air rising over the water.

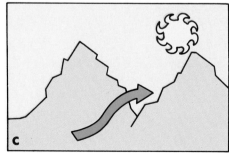

Figure C: A valley breeze occurs when daytime heating of mountain slopes expands the air above them and cooler, heavier air flows up from the valley to replace the rising mountain air.

Figure D: A mountain breeze occurs when cool, dense air slides down the mountainside at night, to replace the warmer, lighter air rising in the valley below.

Watching clouds change, checking wind direction, and noting whether a barometer is falling or rising are key steps in forecasting weather. Opposite, wispy cirrus clouds, drifting above a mixture of dense altocumulus and altostratus clouds, are lit by the sunrise. If they are followed by lower and thicker clouds, a steadily falling barometer, and wind from the south or east, you could forecast rain followed by warmer temperature, higher humidity, and a southwest wind.

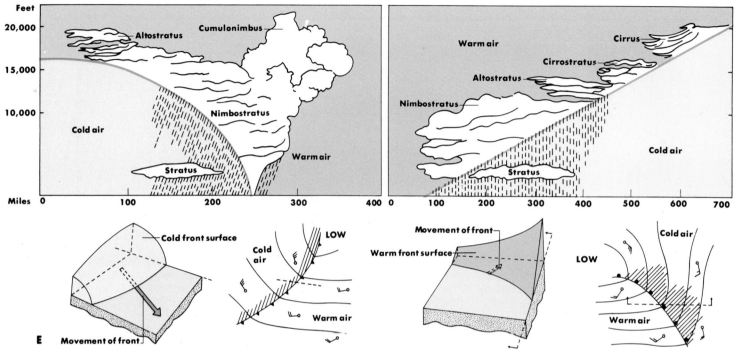

Figure E: Boundaries called fronts occur where air masses of differing temperatures meet. Cold air pushes under lighter warm air when a cold front advances (top left). Or warm air slides up and over denser cold air when a warm front advances (top right). The cloud heights, formations, and distances from the front help forecast which type of front is coming and when it will arrive. How cold and warm fronts appear in perspective and on a weather map is also shown (below left and right).

Answers to that puzzle had to wait until instruments were invented that could measure atmospheric characteristics. Wind vanes and rain gauges had been in use since ancient times. But it wasn't until Galileo invented a thermometer for measuring air temperature in 1607, and his pupil Torricelli a barometer for measuring atmospheric pressure in 1643, that the study of weather became a science. This study was called meteorology (from the Greek *meteorologia*, meaning a discourse on things high in the heavens). Instruments for determining humidity, measuring the expansion and contraction of sheep's wool or human hair as moisture changed in the air, soon followed. Wind speed had long been estimated from its effect on sails, flags, smoke, and even how fast something like thistledown traveled. But it wasn't until the 1800s that a system was developed for correlating wind speed with the effect it had on objects; it was called the Beaufort scale (page 2741), and it is still used today.

With these instruments to measure atmospheric characteristics, the study of weather became quite popular. Thomas Jefferson bought his first thermometer while he was writing the Declaration of Independence and his first barometer shortly after the Declaration was signed. Jefferson, George Washington, James Madison, and Benjamin Franklin all kept records of the weather. In 1777 and 1778, Jefferson and the president of William and Mary College recorded simultaneous weather observations in different locations, the first in America. They had become aware that weather doesn't happen in just one place but travels from one location to another. This is the first rule a forecaster learns.

How Weather Travels

Fortunately, weather travels in patterns forecasters can track. Because the air surrounding the earth is a patchwork quilt of different air masses, each with about the same temperature and moisture throughout its length and width, forecasters can identify these masses and make predictions based on their movements. An air mass from a polar land region will, for example, be cold and dry with high barometric pressure. An air mass from tropical waters will be warm and moist, with a low barometric pressure. When cold and warm air masses meet they do not mix freely (Figure E). Rather, they establish a boundary line known as a front, indicated by

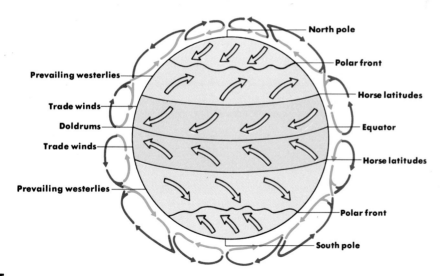

F

Figure F: Hot equatorial air rises and moves toward the poles, while cold polar air is moving along the surface toward the equator, starting the massive flow of air currents surrounding the earth. But air currents aloft are turned eastward and air currents at the surface are turned westward by the earth's rotation, creating the trade winds and prevailing westerlies.

the dark, heavy lines on weather maps (Figure E and page 2750). Most major weather changes occur near such fronts. A front often brings rain and snow, and changes in temperature, air pressure, humidity, and wind direction.

As Figure F shows, vertical air currents created by the sun's heat are converted into spinning winds by the earth's rotation. These global winds pull air masses from the area where they are formed and start them traveling around the earth. In temperate zones, they generally travel from west to east. A common pattern of frontal movement in North America is a cold, high-pressure air mass, followed by a warm front, a warm air mass, a cold front, and another cold air mass, all moving from west to east. The cold air masses have winds that move clockwise around a center of high pressure, called highs. The areas where warm and cold fronts meet have winds that move counterclockwise around a center of low pressure and are called lows. Lows include both warm and cold fronts, and produce most major weather changes.

Luckily for forecasters, both warm and cold fronts travel in the same general direction (from west to east in North America, for example), and they announce their coming in advance by changes in clouds, winds, and air pressure. Certain types of thickening clouds and a steadily falling barometer indicate a warm front is coming. An overcast with rain or snow may begin well before the warm front arrives and continue until the front has passed. The area between a warm and a cold front will be warmer than the air that preceded it or will follow it; skies may clear, but the barometer will show little or no change. Then comes the cold front, often with towering clouds and storms (sometimes violent) accompanying its passage. But behind that cold front is the high with fair weather, a rising barometer, brisker winds, cooler air, and clearing, sunny skies.

To forecast these frontal movements, you need instruments that measure changes in the weather elements, plus an awareness of different cloud formations. An introduction to clouds is in the photographs on pages 2738 and 2739. The instruments you need are: a barometer to measure air pressure; a thermometer to take air temperature; a psychrometer to determine humidity; a wind vane to show wind direction; and an anemometer to measure wind speed. A rain gauge to record the amount of rainfall and a nephoscope to show the direction of cloud movement are also helpful.

You can buy such equipment, but part of the fun of weather forecasting is in making your own instruments, as shown on pages 2740 through 2745. While not as precise as commercial instruments, they serve many amateur forecasters well, as demonstrated on pages 2746 through 2751.

CRAFTNOTES: TYPICAL CLOUD FORMS

Cirrostratus filosus, if it follows cirrus and is followed by altostratus or altocumulus and a falling barometer, may signal an approaching warm front with rain or snow.

The break that lets the sun through and the ragged edges around the break identify this as stratocumulus rather than nimbostratus. Rain or snow is not likely.

Cirrus is above and fragments of stratocumulus below, a combination that may appear toward sunset when heat dissipates. It does not signal major weather changes.

A sheet of cirrostratus is turning into lower, thicker altostratus. If nimbostratus clouds follow and the barometer falls steadily, expect the steady rain preceding a warm front.

The high clouds are wispy cirrus, advancing ahead of the altostratus on the horizon. If the barometer falls steadily and clouds thicken, expect a warm front.

Low, ragged cumulus is in front of the altostratus, which is moving away. High winds are breaking up the cumulus, a sign that weather may improve.

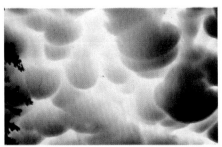

This rare mammato-cumulus, with pendulous masses hanging from the cloud base, is associated with severe thunderstorms and sometimes precedes tornadoes.

Under some faint, high cirrus is a blend of puffy altocumulus and fibrous altostratus. If followed by nimbostratus, this could signal an approaching warm front.

The base of a large dark cumulonimbus cloud is approaching with rain showers preceding it. It could signal the approach of a cold front or a heavy local thundershower.

Although this has the even texture of some drizzle-producing stratus clouds, it is a haze often found near the horizon at sunset in fair weather. Expect no sudden changes.

Cirrus (above right) and broken cumulus (below) mark the breakup of a cumulonimbus cloud. So many clouds form from cumulonimbus that they are called cloud factories.

Some cirrus mixed with altostratus provides a colorful sunset and suggests improving weather. The same combination seen at sunrise might signal a warm front approaching.

AND THE WEATHER THEY MAY FORETELL

These swelling cumulus accompany fair weather that follows a cold front. If they do not build into cumulonimbus or another cloud form fair weather should continue.

Altocumulus (right) and altostratus (left) have followed an afternoon shower and the breakup of the cumulonimbus clouds that brought the storm. Weather is clearing.

Stratocumulus vesperalis is a form of stratocumulus that may appear in the evening and then dissipate. It does not signal a major change in the weather.

Cumulus clouds such as these are associated with the highs that follow a cold front and often appear between warm and cold fronts. They signal fair weather.

Cumulus clouds will often flatten out in the late afternoon and dissipate by evening. They do not signal the movement of a front that would bring a major weather change.

Nimbostratus is in the background with a low fog approaching in the foreground. Both of these can be signs that a slow-moving, stable warm front is arriving.

The base of a cumulonimbus cloud marks a passing cold front. Cooler weather, with brisk winds and sunny or partly sunny skies, should follow the front's passage.

Two waterspouts, which are tornadoes that occur over water, emerge from the base of a cumulonimbus cloud that developed violent rotary winds associated with tornadoes.

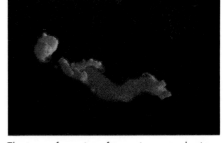

The tops of a series of towering cumulonimbus are just visible in the sun as this stormy cold front passes by. The same clouds accompany local thunderstorms.

All these are cumulus clouds, but those on the right are beginning to build into what could become cumulonimbus clouds that often produce local thundershowers.

Stratus clouds such as these can precede some slow-moving warm fronts with low winds. Stratus may produce drizzle but not the rain accompanying nimbostratus.

Cumulus is in the foreground at left with patches of altocumulus in the background. Expect no major changes unless the altocumulus thickens into a continuous layer.

Making weather instruments

There are few rules you need to follow in making simple weather instruments. Most can be made from found objects or scrap. In any of the following projects, feel free to substitute other materials for any you do not have. I do recommend that you buy commercial thermometers, since making accurately calibrated ones is difficult.

Wind Vane
The wind vane shown in photograph 1 and in silhouette on page 2735 consists of three dowels for the arrow and direction-marker arms; a wood scrap cut into a triangle shape for the arrowhead; an arrow tail cut from a straight-sided tin can; one or two small, round fishing weights to add weight to the front of the arrow; four direction markers (N,E,S, and W); a 3-inch piece of straight coat-hanger wire; a short length of small, rigid metal or plastic tubing; and a broomstick or mop handle. The length of the dowels is not critical, but they should be thick enough so you can cut slots in them for mounting the arrow tail and the direction markers. The wooden arrowhead should be thick enough so you can drill a hole in it for the arrow dowel. You can buy direction markers at a hardware store or cut them from a tin can, thin wood, or plastic. You will also need: a thin-bladed saw; tin snips; small clamps; a ruler; compass; protractor; drill; drill bits the diameter of the dowels, the tubing and the coat-hanger wire; and waterproof glue.

Cut the arrow dowel to length; the one shown is 12 inches. Saw a ½-inch slot in one end to hold the arrow tail. Draw a triangle with two equal sides on a wood scrap, making the base about 2¼ inches and the height about 2¾ inches. Saw out the triangle, and drill a hole 1 inch deep in the center of its base, the same diameter as that of the arrow dowel (photograph 2). Draw an arrow tail that is larger than the arrowhead (to catch more wind), trace it on a straight-sided tin can, and cut it out with tin snips. Use glue to fix the tail into the slot cut for it. Tap a brad through dowel and tail to anchor this joint, and clamp it while the glue dries.

Drop one or two small fishing weights into the hole drilled in the arrowhead, apply glue to the front end of the arrow dowel, and press on the arrowhead. Now balance the arrow on the edge of a ruler held in a vise, and mark the place where the vane is balanced (photograph 3). Drill a vertical hole for the coat-hanger wire through the dowel at this point.

Cut the two dowels that will serve as directional pointers to equal lengths. Saw slits in each end of each dowel to hold the directional markers. Drill one hole the size of the dowels through the broomstick about 1¼ inch down from its tip, keeping your drill at right angles to the broomstick. Drill a second hole 2 inches down from the tip and at right angles to the first (photograph 4). To make sure the second hole is at right angles to the first, trace the tip of the broomstick on lined paper; then use a protractor to mark the 0-, 90-, 180-, and 270-degree points on that circle. Hold the tip of the broomstick on its circle and align the 0- and 180-degree marks with the centers of the hole already drilled. The 90- and 270-degree points will tell you where to drill the second hole.

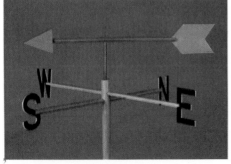

1: Wind vane consists of dowel, arrowhead cut from scrap wood, and arrow tail cut from straight-sided tin can. When assembled these mount on piece of tubing inserted in broomstick, with a piece of coat-hanger wire running through dowel into the center of the broomstick.

2: After drilling a hole in the base of the wind vane's arrowhead, test the fit of the arrow shaft. Then drop one or two small fishing weights in the hole before you glue the shaft in place.

3: With the arrowhead and a sheet-metal tail attached to the arrow shaft, find the point on the shaft where the vane will balance on the edge of a ruler. Mark that point for drilling.

4: After drilling holes through the broomstick for the directional pointer dowels, cut slots in the ends of the dowels, fit the directional markers in them, and glue in place.

Fit the directional-marker dowels through their holes and glue them there so they project an equal distance on all sides (photograph 4). Slip the N, S, E, and W markers in the slits cut for them in the ends of the dowels; glue in place and clamp until the glue dries. Drill a hole the diameter of the coat-hanger wire and 1½ inches deep in the center of the broomstick tip. In the first hole, drill a second hole ½ inch deep and the diameter of the section of rigid plastic or metal tubing. The vane could pivot directly on top of the broomstick, but the tubing raises the vane enough to ensure that it will clear the direction markers as it swings around. Finish all wooden parts with two coats of wood preservative, or a sealer and several coats of paint.

When you are ready to place the vane in your yard, away from any obstructions that might interrupt the flow of wind, drive the broomstick into the ground, making sure it is vertical. Using a compass, turn the broomstick until the N is pointed north. Fit the tubing into its hole, and slip the coat-hanger wire through the hole in the arrow, the tubing, and into the broomstick.

In noting wind direction, remember that winds are named for the direction from which they blow, the direction toward which the wind vane arrow will point.

Hand-held Anemometer

You can estimate wind speed by using the Beaufort scale (below). Or you can get a more accurate measurement with a hand-held anemometer (photograph 5) or a pole-mounted anemometer (page 2742). The hand-held anemometer is made from an 8⅛-by-12-inch piece of ⅜-inch plywood, a 2-by-9-inch strip of heavy copper, brass, or steel, and a ⅛-inch bolt 3 inches long with nuts and washers to contain the metal strip while letting it swing freely up the marked scale as the wind blows against it.

Use a coping saw to cut out the plywood shape (Figure G). Draw a line down the center of the straight arm and drill a hole for the bolt on this center line, 1 inch from the top of this arm. Tap a small nail into the center line 7½ inches down from the top of the arm. This will serve as a stop for the copper strip and the zero point on the speed scale you will make. Insert the bolt through its hole, using nuts and washers at the bolt head and on both sides of the wood (photograph 6). Fold the metal strip over the bolt so that 6¾ inches of it extend down the straight vertical arm and about 2 inches down the opposite side of the bolt. Make sure this strip will swing freely across the curved arm. Trace the outline of the curved arm on cardboard or heavy paper, cut this out, and glue it to the face of the curved arm.

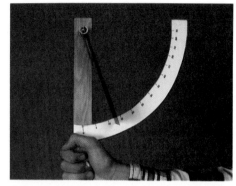

5: As wind pushes up the heavy metal strip of this hand-held anemometer, the scale indicates the speed at which the wind is blowing.

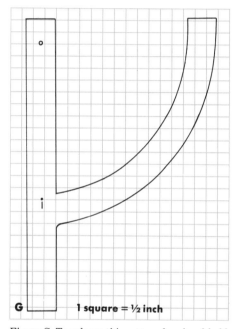

G   1 square = ½ inch

Figure G: To enlarge this pattern for a hand-held anemometer, draw a grid of ½-inch squares. Copy this design onto the larger grid, one square at a time. Cut out the pattern, trace it on ⅜-inch plywood, and saw it out.

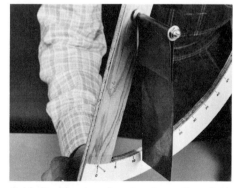

6: A bolt with nuts and washers keeps the metal strip anchored while letting it swing across the scale on the curved arm; a nail serves as a stop at the zero point.

BEAUFORT SCALE FOR ESTIMATING WIND SPEED*

Beaufort number	Miles per hour	Type of wind	Identifying signs
0	Less than 1	Calm	Smoke rises vertically.
1	1 to 3	Light air	Smoke drift shows direction but wind vanes do not respond.
2	4 to 7	Light breeze	Wind vanes move; leaves rustle; wind is felt on the face.
3	8 to 12	Gentle breeze	Leaves and small twigs keep moving. Light flags are extended.
4	13 to 18	Moderate breeze	Small branches and loose papers move about; dust is raised.
5	19 to 24	Fresh breeze	Small trees in leaf sway.
6	25 to 31	Strong breeze	Large branches start moving; wires strung outdoors whistle.
7	32 to 38	Near gale	Whole trees are in motion; it is hard to walk against the wind.
8	39 to 46	Gale	Twigs break from trees. Moving vehicles are affected.
9	47 to 54	Strong gale	Slight damage to buildings—roof tiles are blown off and signs blown down.
10	55 to 63	Storm	Much building damage; trees are uprooted.
11	64 to 72	Violent storm	Widespread damage.
12	73 and over	Hurricane	The extreme destruction that is associated with tornadoes and hurricanes.

*Most professional weather maps (page 2750) use a slightly different division of wind speeds.

7: In a pole-mounted anemometer, the spool section with cups attached slips over a section of metal tubing mounted atop the broomstick. A washer between the spool and the broomstick reduces friction so the cups can spin freely.

8: Thin dowels fit through holes in plastic cups and into holes in a center spool. The cross of black tape on one cup makes it easier to count the revolutions as the cups spin on the broomstick.

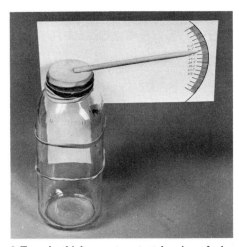

9: To make this barometer, stretch a piece of rubber or impermeable plastic wrap tightly over a wide-mouthed bottle, and hold it in place with rubber bands. Glue a dowel pointer to the rubber; then cut an L-shaped piece of cardboard and attach it to the bottle behind the pointer. Calibrate the scale with the aid of barometric pressures reported on your local radio.

Calibrating by Car

To calibrate the anemometer, have someone drive you along a nearly deserted road on a calm day. Hold the anemometer out the window with the wide side of the copper strip facing the wind created by the car's movement. Have the driver hold steady speeds of 5, then 10, then 15, then 20 miles per hour and so on, and, on the curved arm, mark the position of the copper strip at each speed. (The marks should be closer together at the outer end of the scale.) If higher speeds push the strip beyond the end of the scale, you can use a heavier gauge of metal or attach short, heavy bolts and nuts near the bottom of the strip to give extra weight. Coat the wood with preservative or use sealer and paint.

Pole-mounted Anemometer

If you mount an anemometer on a broomstick beside a wind vane (photograph 7 and silhouette, page 2735), you can check both wind speed and direction by watching the instruments through the window. The pole-mounted anemometer shown is made of four cups; four lengths of dowel ⅛ inch in diameter, each 7 inches long; half a wooden spool 1½ inches in diameter; a 3-inch length of rigid tubing ¼ inch in diameter; a washer; black electrical tape; and a broomstick on which to mount the instrument. As the cups, I used halves of egg-shaped plastic containers, but plastic drinking cups will also work. The cups should be light. A ⅞-inch-thick section of 1½-inch dowel can be used in place of the spool, if you drill a hole through the center of the dowel section.

Saw a section of the spool ¾ inch thick. Trace around the spool and use a protractor to mark 0-, 90-, 180-, and 270-degree positions on the circle. Then place the spool on the circle and mark these positions on the spool. Drill ⅛-inch holes through the side of the spool toward the center, stopping just short of the center hole.

Using lined paper and a compass, draw a circle the diameter of one of the cups, placing the center of the circle on a line. Place a cup on the circle, and mark it where the line intersects its edge on either side. Make holes slightly smaller than the dowel that will fit through them, locating them above each mark and ⅜ inch in from the edge of the cup on either side. If the cup is plastic, these holes can be melted through the plastic with a heated awl or ice pick.

Cut the four dowels and fit one end of each through the two holes in a cup and the other end into a hole in the spool (photograph 8). Apply glue to the dowels and the holes. You may need to enlarge the holes slightly with sandpaper or a small round file, but make sure the fit is snug. The open side of each cup must be at right angles to the ground with each facing so it will catch the same wind as the spool spins.

Cut a 3-inch section of rigid plastic or metal tubing that will fit through the hole in the center of the spool (photograph 7), using tubing small enough to let the spool spin freely on it. Enlarge the hole in the spool if necessary. Then drill a hole the diameter of this tubing in the center of one end of the broomstick.

Drive the broomstick into the ground in your yard, locating it near the weather vane so that you can read both at the same time. Make sure the broomstick is vertical. Fit the tubing into its hole in the broomstick and glue in place. When the glue has dried, slip a washer over the tubing to minimize friction, and slip the spool-and-cup assembly over the tubing.

Calibrating the Anemometer

Attach strips of black tape to form a cross on the back of one cup (photograph 7). This will help you count the number of revolutions the spinning cups make. Cut a short section of dowel for a handle, drill a hole the diameter of the tubing in one end of the dowel, and mount the anemometer. Then check its revolutions against an automobile speedometer, as described above. In this case, however, count the number of turns made in 30 seconds at different speeds, and record them. Then make a graph with speeds marked along the bottom and the number of turns up one side. Connect the plotted points, and you can tell how fast the wind is blowing at any given number of turns.

Bottle Barometer

For the barometer shown (photograph 9), you need: a wide-mouthed bottle; a piece of thin rubber or impermeable plastic wrap; a 6¼-inch length of 3/16-inch dowel; a shirt cardboard; and four or five strong rubber bands. When the rubber or plastic is bound tightly onto the top of the bottle, the differences in pressure between the air trapped inside the bottle and the changing pressure outside will cause the rubber to push out or sink in. This moves a dowel pointer attached to the rubber.

Cut a section of rubber large enough to cover the top of the bottle and extend down onto the bottle neck on all sides. Stretch this tightly, and hold it in place with rubber bands around the bottle neck. The rubber must be taut and wrinkle free. Using sandpaper, sharpen one end of the dowel, and slightly flatten 5/8 to 3/4 inch of one side at the other end. Dust the dowel, put glue on the flattened section, and fix this to the rubber covering the bottle. The dowel should extend no more than one-third to one-half the distance from the edge of the bottle to the center of its opening. Use a large rubber band to clamp this joint while the glue dries (photograph 10).

Cut an L-shaped piece of cardboard so one leg can be fixed to the side of the bottle with rubber bands, while the other extends behind the dowel pointer. Draw an arc on the cardboard behind the tip of the pointer; you will watch the movement of the pointer across the arc.

Calibrating the Barometer

Place the barometer in a room where the temperature will remain constant, perhaps the basement, in a location where you can view the pointer at eye level under the same source of light at all times. Listen to a local radio weather report to get the current barometer reading. Mark the reading at the point where the barometer pointer (or its shadow) crosses the arc you drew. Repeat the procedure at intervals for a week or two, entering new notations each time you hear a new reading. (Most barometer changes are slight, usually moving between 29 and 30.5 inches in temperate zones.) But differences in altitude can change the scale, as can the deeply falling barometer readings associated with some major storms. So make your scale somewhat wider than the readings you obtained from radio reports. With these readings as plotting points, divide the arc into a scale, filling in intervening readings in tenths and hundredths. You will need to remove the cardboard from the bottle to draw the scale; be sure you put it back in the same position so that the pointer indicates the same reading that it did when you removed the cardboard.

If the barometer does not seem to be responding to weather changes as it should, the rubber or plastic cover may not be air tight. Bind a new piece of rubber tightly around the top with rubber bands.

Combined Thermometer and Psychrometer

The instrument shown in photograph 11 does double duty. The thermometer without the wet cotton wick attached to its bulb reads the air temperature. And the difference between the readings of the dry- and wet-bulb thermometers, when interpreted with the table on page 2744, reveals the relative humidity. When the combination is used to determine relative humidity, the instrument is known as a psychrometer; it is more accurate than the old hygrometers that relied on the expansion and contraction of human hairs to measure humidity.

Select two low-cost commercial thermometers that register identical readings in the store. Use a single-edged razor blade to cut off the folded top of a half-gallon milk carton, and wash the container with warm water and detergent. Cover it with plain paper if you would like a neat appearance. Attach the thermometers to two adjoining sides of the milk carton with rubber bands. Cut a 3-inch section of wide cotton shoelace and boil it for five minutes. Use the razor blade to cut a slot 1/16 inch wide and 3/4 inch long, about ½ inch below one of the thermometer bulbs. Slip one end of the shoelace over this bulb and tuck the other end through the slot into the carton. Fill the carton with water to a level just below the slot so the free end of the shoelace is in the water. The wet shoelace, acting as a wick, will draw water through the slot and up over the bulb of the thermometer.

In summer when the windows are open, the humidity indoors and out will be about the same, so you can keep the psychrometer indoors. When the windows are closed, place it in an outside box, shielded from the sun and rain but open to the air on one side. An ideal location is just outside a ground-level basement window.

To determine the humidity, note the readings of the two thermometers. If the instrument is indoors where there is no breeze, fan the wet bulb with a piece of

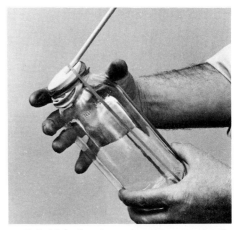

10: To hold the dowel onto the rubber covering the top of the bottle while the glue dries, place a rubber band over the bottle lengthwise.

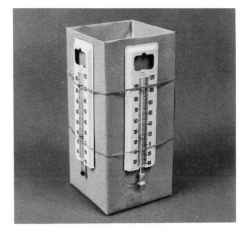

11: With this combination thermometer/psychrometer, air temperature readings can be obtained from the thermometer with the exposed bulb at left. Humidity can be determined by subtracting the reading of the wet-bulb thermometer at right (its bulb is covered by a shoelace wick) from the readings of the dry (exposed) bulb thermometer at left, then referring to the table on page 2744.

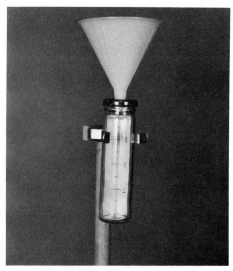

12: This rain gauge is held erect with a thick dowel that has a broom clip mounted on scrap wood on top. The straight-sided olive bottle, with a plastic funnel inserted through its top, has a paper scale taped to its back that is calibrated to measure tenths of an inch of rain.

cardboard or an electric fan for half a minute; then take its reading. Subtract the wet-bulb reading from the dry-bulb reading. Then apply the air temperature reading (dry bulb) and the difference between the dry-and wet-bulb readings to determine the relative humidity given in the table below.

Although the alcohol in the thermometers won't freeze at most temperate zone winter temperatures, the water in the carton will; so take the instrument inside during below-freezing weather.

Rain Gauge

After you have determined how much rain has fallen a few times, you can begin to correlate rainfall with the types of fronts that move over your area, making you a better forecaster. Any straight-sided container can be used to measure rainfall; after the rain ends, put a dry ruler down to the bottom and see how many inches or fractions of an inch are wet. If the container is transparent, you can read the water level on a ruler through the side. But most rainfalls amount to only small fractions of an inch, and it is difficult to take precise readings of such small amounts with a ruler. For that reason, most rain gauges are designed to multiply the effect of small rainfalls by using a wide-mouthed funnel to direct rain into a small container (photograph 12).

To make the gauge shown, you need: a 15-inch length of dowel 1 inch in diameter; a narrow, straight-sided olive bottle with a cap; a plastic funnel with a 3½-to 4-inch opening at the top; a broom clip; a scrap of wood ¾ inch square on which the broom clip is mounted; an inch-wide strip of paper as long as the bottle is tall; transparent tape; glue; and small nails or screws. With the bottle-top well clamped, drill a hole in its center slightly larger than the small tip of the funnel; press the plastic funnel tip through this hole until you achieve a firm, tight fit.

RELATIVE HUMIDITY TABLE

Air temperature, Fahrenheit (dry-bulb reading)	Difference between dry- and wet-bulb thermometer readings													
	1°	2°	3°	4°	6°	8°	10°	12°	14°	16°	18°	20°	25°	30°
0	67	33	1											
5	73	46	20											
10	78	56	34	13										
15	82	64	46	29										
20	85	70	55	40	12									
25	87	74	62	49	25	1								
30	89	78	67	56	36	16								
35	91	81	72	63	45	27	10							
40	92	83	75	68	52	37	22	7						
45	93	86	78	71	57	44	31	18	6					
50	93	87	80	74	61	49	38	27	16	5				
55	94	88	82	76	65	54	43	33	23	14	5			
60	94	89	83	78	68	58	48	39	30	21	13	5		
65	95	90	85	80	70	61	52	44	35	27	20	12		
70	95	90	86	81	72	64	55	48	40	33	25	19	3	
75	96	91	86	82	74	66	58	51	44	37	30	24	9	
80	96	91	87	83	75	68	61	54	47	41	35	29	15	3
85	96	92	88	84	76	70	63	56	50	44	38	32	20	8
90	96	92	89	85	78	71	65	58	52	47	41	36	24	13
95	96	93	89	86	79	72	66	60	54	49	44	38	27	17
100	96	93	89	86	80	73	68	62	56	51	46	41	30	21

You can also determine the humidity when it is between the figures shown in this chart. For example, assume 97 degrees is the air temperature (dry bulb) and the difference between the dry-bulb and wet-bulb readings is 20 degrees. Use this formula:

$$\frac{97-95}{100-95} = \frac{x}{41-38} \quad \text{or} \quad \frac{2}{5} = \frac{x}{3} \quad \text{or} \quad x = 1.2$$

Thus, the relative humidity is 38+1.2, or 39, reading to the nearest whole percent.

Point one end of the dowel with a rasp or knife. Nail or screw the wood scrap to the other end, and screw the broom clip to the scrap, using the screw that comes with the clip. Drive the dowel into the ground in an open area.

Calibrating the Gauge

There are two ways to calibrate the gauge. If you have a straight-sided container with an inside diameter the same as the funnel's top inside diameter, pour an inch of water into this container. Then pour this water into the olive bottle. Hold the paper strip beside the olive bottle so the bottom of the strip is even with the inside bottom of the bottle. Make a long mark even with the top of the water. Divide the rest of the strip with long marks the same distance apart as the distance from the end of the strip to the first mark. Then make shorter marks halfway between each of the long marks. Finally, by eye, divide each space between a short and a long mark into five equal portions, making a dot between each portion. The longer marks will represent inches of rain, the shorter marks half-inches, and the dots tenths of an inch. Number the long marks from the bottom up; then glue and tape the paper scale to the outside back of the bottle, with the marks on the inside, so that you can read water levels against the scale.

If you can't find a straight-sided container to match the top of the funnel, set the unmarked gauge outside and wait for a rain. When the rain stops, hold the paper strip beside the bottle and make a long mark matching the level of water in the bottle. Listen for the amount of rainfall announced on the nearest radio station, and label the mark on the strip with that amount. Mark off the same distance on the remainder of the strip as many times as it will repeat. Then, as before, divide the distance between these marks in half and then into five equal portions, making shorter marks and dots. Label each long and short mark with the inches and fractions of an inch it represents. With the scale fixed to the bottle, fit the cap and funnel on the bottle and the bottle into the broom clip. Check the gauge and empty it after each rain. If freezing temperatures and precipitation are forecast, bring the gauge indoors; freezing water could crack the bottle.

Cloud-Movement Nephoscope

Weather vanes near the ground are not always true indicators of wind direction; hills, buildings, and rough terrain may interrupt the wind flow and change its direction. Professional meteorologists send up balloons to check the unobstructed wind movements associated with major weather changes. Instead of a balloon, you can use a nephoscope to do the same job. It consists of a flat, round mirror and a cardboard directional marker that fits around the mirror (photograph 13). The movement of clouds reflected in the mirror shows the direction of unobstructed higher winds that are pushing the clouds.

Cut a square of cardboard 2 inches larger than the diameter of the mirror. Draw lines dividing the cardboard in half from top to bottom and side to side. Place a protractor on the cardboard so that its 0-, 90-, 180- and 270-degree marks (representing north, east, south, and west) coincide with the lines drawn. Add marks at the 45-, 135-, 225- and 315-degree positions (representing northeast, southeast, southwest, and northwest). Extend these marks out toward the edges of the cardboard so they will be easy to read.

Center the mirror on the cardboard, trace around it, and cut out the traced circle. Glue a small circle of paper (from a paper punch) onto the exact center of the mirror, where lines joining north and south and east and west would cross. Place the mirror outdoors on a small table or box, in a clear area where it will reflect the sky. Make sure the mirror is level; use small shims of thin wood or cardboard to level it if necessary.

Since winds are named for the direction from which they blow, if you position the nephoscope so that its south mark is facing north and its west mark is facing east, a cloud moving over these marks will indicate the direction of the wind. Use a compass to position the instrument precisely. Then watch for clouds moving across the mirror. Pick out a distinctive part of a cloud (a hump or a curl on its edge) that will pass over the dot in the center of the mirror. Follow this feature from the center dot to the edge of the mirror, and read the direction indicated as the direction of the wind pushing the cloud.

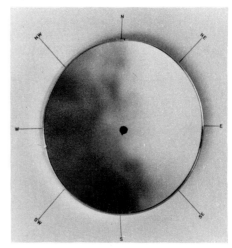

13: Movement of clouds across the mirror of this nephoscope shows the direction of the wind that is pushing the clouds. It may not be the same as the wind close to the ground, which could be diverted by hills, trees, and other obstructions.

Aches and adages

Tempers rise in hot, muggy, overcast weather; spirits improve with cool, dry, sunny weather. But can the physical reactions of the human body help in forecasting? There is evidence they can. The falling barometer and rising humidity associated with impending weather changes can be felt in the form of stiff aching joints, particularly by people prone to arthritis. The problem is that other physical factors can also start the joints complaining. So a check of your weather instruments may be more reliable than Grandpa's grousing.

How reliable are the old weather sayings such as "red sky at night, sailor's delight (implying clear weather); red sky in the morning, sailors take warning (implying storms)." That particular adage is right about 70 percent of the time. Other adages may be less reliable. Too often, their accuracy depends on where you live and the pattern and speed of warm and cold fronts moving across your area.

Environmental Projects
Using weather instruments

It is the *changes* in weather-instrument readings that tell what the future weather will be like. Keeping a continuing record, like the weather log below, will show you at a glance what changes are occurring. Take readings twice a day (more often if you can) and at the same time each day. This will minimize the effect of such normal variations as the daily rise and fall in temperature or the regular development of sea or valley breezes (page 2734).

Before you try forecasting major weather changes, use your instruments to measure the regular local changes that occur during several clear, sunny days with calm or light winds. How much does the temperature rise during the day and fall in the evening? What changes in humidity accompany this rise and fall in temperature? (Normally, minimum humidity accompanies maximum temperature during the day, and maximum humidity the minimum temperature at night.) There is also a slight daily variation in atmospheric pressure—about .03 inch in temperate zones and .10 inch in the tropics—with maximum readings at about 10 A.M. and 2 A.M., minimums at 6 P.M. 5 A.M. If your area has local sea and land breezes, or mountain and valley breezes, measure their strength. Depending on their direction and intensity, such local winds can strengthen or weaken the winds associated with frontal movements across your area. Cumulus clouds also have a local pattern of growing and disappearing on sunny days, though sometimes they build up enough to produce local thunderstorms (page 2749).

The local variations—often slight—rarely have a major effect on frontal weather movements. But by learning what they are, you won't confuse them with changes accompanying the massive frontal movements that you want to predict. Local variations may also explain why your readings may not agree with those shown for your area on official weather maps.

Forecasting the Weather Changes

With a weather log developed and a knowledge of highs, lows, and warm and cold fronts (pages 2736 and 2737), you are ready to try forecasting the fronts' arrivals and the weather that will accompany and follow them. First check your log entries on clouds. If you have noted wispy cirrus clouds followed by cirrostratus, and then

WEATHER LOG

Date	Time	Cloud types; 10ths of sky covered*	Barometer	Wind direction	Wind speed	Temperature	Humidity	Rain or snow	Forecast
5/2/75	8 am	Ci-3	30.30	WSW	2	45	47	None	Still in high but Ci may mean low is coming. No rain for next few hours but may cloud up.
5/2/75	2 pm	Cs-7	30.17	SSW	15	56	42	None	Thickening Cs, sharp barometer fall, wind backing toward S mean warm front, rain likely.
5/2/75	9 pm	St-10	30.02	S	9	54	64	Rain	Rain and overcast confirm slow-moving warm front. More rain in next few hours.
5/3/75	8 am	Ac-9	29.72	SE	11	59	78	None	Rain recorded at 11 p.m. Wind shift to SE means warm front close. Some clearing with higher temperatures by afternoon.
5/3/75	2 pm	As-6	29.68	SW	9	70	51	None	Wind shift to SW and clearing skies mean warm front has passed, cold front may be coming, followed by clearing and cooler weather.
5/3/75	9 pm	None	29.86	NW	24	59	42	None	Rising barometer, falling temperature, clear skies, wind shift to NW confirm cold front passage. Fair, cooler weather should continue.

*For a complete list of symbols used for clouds on weather maps, write to the Superintendent of Documents, Washington, D. C., 20402, asking for pamphlet NOAA/PA 71012 on clouds.

14: If high, wispy cirrus clouds are followed by this combination of cirrocumulus on top, with cirrostratus below them, this can be your first clue to a warm front coming with rain or snow.

15: Another combination that may be a forerunner of an approaching warm front has delicate cirrus on top, with thick altocumulus developing below, suggesting that the front's approach may be rapid.

16: If thick nimbostratus clouds move in at lower levels, following altocumulus or altostratus and a falling barometer, you can expect rain to begin soon as the warm front nears.

17: Stormy cumulonimbus clouds are often forerunners of a fast-moving cold front that will bring rain and gusty winds, possibly accompanied by thunder, lightning, or even hail.

thicker, lower altostratus or altocumulus (photographs 14 and 15) it is likely that the warm front of a low is several hundred miles to the west of you and moving in your direction.

Confirm the warning the clouds give by checking your weather log readings for wind direction and barometric pressure. If the wind is from the south or southeast and the barometer is falling steadily, a low is coming from the west or northwest and its center will pass near or to the north of you in 12 to 24 hours. If the wind is from the east or northeast and the barometer is falling steadily, the low is coming from the south or southwest and its center will pass near or to the south or east of you in 12 to 24 hours. In temperate zones, lows normally travel 400 miles a day in summer, 500 in winter, though some move as slowly as 100 and others as fast as 800 miles a day. If the barometer's fall is rapid, the low is moving quickly, and the storms accompanying the passage of its fronts will be more intense. A good forecast at this point would be rain or, in winter with the air temperature below freezing, possible snow.

Warm Front Arriving

Another check on the clouds may show that nimbostratus clouds (or sometimes, cumulonimbus) have covered the sky as the low's warm front gets closer (photographs 16 and 17). (If cumulonimbus clouds show, expect a stormy frontal passage.) Rain or snow may begin to fall and it may continue until the warm front passes. Very low stratus clouds may move in and hide higher clouds. Then, as the warm front passes, the winds will shift to the south or southwest, temperature will rise, humidity may increase, skies may clear or show scattered clouds, and the barometer will show little change from the last low reading. You are now in the warm air mass between the warm and cold fronts in the low.

18: Stratocumulus clouds frequently appear after a cold-front passage to be replaced by the fair weather cumulus and the clearing skies associated with high pressure areas.

Cold Front Coming

The next weather change to look for is the cold front that usually follows the warm front in a low. The first sign of it may be thickening clouds with cumulonimbus building up to the west or northwest (photographs 17 and 19). If the barometer holds to its last low reading, humidity increases, and southwest winds begin to quicken as the cumulonimbus clouds approach, the cold front is not far away. A good forecast at this stage would be the possibility of brief showers, followed by more intense thundershowers or squalls as the front arrives. This in turn would be followed by a rising barometer, a drop in temperature and humidity, strong winds shifting to the northwest, and the clearing skies associated with fair weather (photograph 18). You would then be in the high that follows a cold front.

High Moving Over

A high may remain stationary for a day or two or even a week, or it may move on at the average rate for highs of 400 miles a day in summer, 600 miles a day in winter. Since the average high is some 2000 miles in diameter, however, it may take the one you are in some time to pass. You can check its progress in your weather log by watching the barometer, temperature, and wind speed and direction readings. Pressure will rise until the center of the high passes, then will begin to decline. Temperatures and wind speeds tend to fall until the high's center passes, then rise. Wind will usually shift, as the high's center passes, from northwest to southeast.

19: When fair-weather cumulus start to build high (left), as they often do on a hot, muggy afternoon, they are apt to convert into towering cumulonimbus clouds with strong vertical air currents (center). These clouds frequently develop a characteristic anvil shape at the top (right). Quick, drenching thunderstorms and sometimes hail come from such clouds.

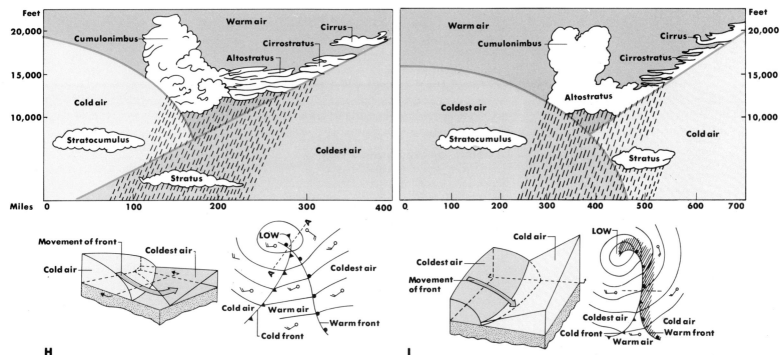

H

Figure H: A fast-moving cold air mass can overtake a slower moving warm front, creating cloud and precipitation patterns associated with a warm front. Air behind the front will be cool but not as cold as the air that preceded it. At the bottom is how such an occluded front looks in perspective and on a weather map.

I

Figure I: If the overtaking air is colder, the occluded front will be a cold-front type and look like this. The sequence of cloud forms accompanying such a front will be higher off the ground, since they form in warm air that has been pushed up by the approaching front. At the bottom is how such a front looks in perspective and on a weather map.

Local Thunderstorms

During the passage of a high and often in the clearing area between a warm and cold front in a low, your forecasts would be for generally fair weather. But keep an eye on the clouds. On a hot, humid day, scattered cumulus may build during the morning and change into towering cumulonimbus clouds by afternoon (photograph 19). These can bring local thunderstorms, with gusty winds and quick, drenching rains. They might not hit in your immediate vicinity but if the clouds move your way and skies become more and more overcast as the clouds build, there is a good chance they will. After the center of a high has passed you, keep checking your weather log for the succession of thickening clouds, steadily falling barometer, and wind changes that signal another low is on the way. It will be along eventually.

While the sequence of lows with their warm and cold fronts, followed by highs, happens often, variations are frequent. Air masses move at different speeds and often overtake each other. This produces what are called occluded fronts and the kind of weather depicted in Figures H and I. Because warm air is pushed high between two masses of cold air, the sequence of clouds associated with the passage of such a front will usually be higher off the ground. Cold air will follow cold air after the frontal storms pass. If the overtaking cold air is colder than the air ahead of the warm front, the occluded front resembles a cold front at the surface. But if the relative temperatures of the cold air masses are reversed, it will resemble a warm front at the surface.

Some fronts pause for awhile, with neither air mass displacing the other. Called stationary fronts, they may resemble a warm front but develop later into either a warm or cold front. After detecting an approaching front, if you find no appreciable changes in your weather log readings, it suggests that a front has become stationary. It will move eventually and changes in the clouds and weather log readings (sometimes sudden) will signal the movement is under way.

Some fronts are too weak to be accompanied by a cloud buildup or sharp changes in weather-instrument readings. A distinct shift in wind direction and slight changes in barometer, humidity, and temperature readings are the best clues to their arrival and passage.

20: The fog in the foreground is forming as warm air moves over cool water. Nimbostratus clouds in the background are associated with the approach of a stable warm front. When the fog moves inland over warmer land, it may lift somewhat and become a stratus cloud.

Fog, a Cloud on the Ground

As a local condition, fog may form whenever warm damp air flows over cool land or water at night or when moist air moves up a slope and condenses. Even on a calm, clear night, the ground sometimes cools rapidly enough to condense water vapor the air above it into fog. Fogs are also associated with the movement of some front and air masses. Expect them in the rainy area accompanying a warm front that has moved in with lowering nimbostratus or stratus clouds and light winds (photograph 20). They also occur where damp polar air formed over the sea moves inland, as it so often does in the Pacific Northwest in summer.

Tornadoes and Waterspouts

Even professional forecasters have difficulty predicting tornadoes and waterspouts (the latter are tornadoes that form over water). But there are clues as to when they may occur. When a severe cold front suddenly collides with a mass of hot, humid air, the hot air trying to escape aloft acquires a rotary motion that may increase in intensity until the deadly funnel is formed. The same towering cumulonimbus clouds that bring severe storms, lightning, and hail can mark the beginning of a tornado's development. When portions of the base of the cloud start extending toward the ground, as in the mammato-cumulus clouds pictured on page 2738, a tornado may follow. If winds show an ever tighter rotary motion and part of the base of the cloud starts to acquire a funnel shape reaching down toward the ground, the tornado is forming. (It can't be properly called one until it touches ground.) The funnel may be light in color at first. Then, if over land, it will steadily darken as it whirls dust and debris from the ground upward in winds traveling at several hundred miles an hour.

In the United States tornadoes occur most frequently in April, May, and June, and least frequently in December and January. When tornadoes increase in frequency in February, most of them occur over the central gulf states. During March the center of maximum frequency moves to the southeast states and reaches a peak there in April. In May, the southern plains states have the most tornadoes and in June, most occur in the northern plains and Great Lakes area as far east as western New York. But no states are immune from them at any season. Tornadoes form most readily during the warm hours of the day, but they also occur at night. Forecasters watch for them closely when surges of hot moist southern air and cold dry northern air are likely to meet suddenly in late winter, spring, or early summer.

Hurricanes

Violent hurricanes are believed to form when a low pressure area disturbs the relatively docile easterly trade winds flowing over tropical seas. Winds pile up, carrying warm moist air as high as 40,000 feet before the air loses its heat and moisture and descends. But the earth's rotation turns these rising columns of air into spinning cylinders, circling a center of relatively still air (the eye of the hurricane). These spinning cylinders draw more warm, moist air up from the sea, strengthening the whirling winds. When the hurricane moves over land or cooler water, it loses the warm, moist sea air that energized it, and soon dies out.

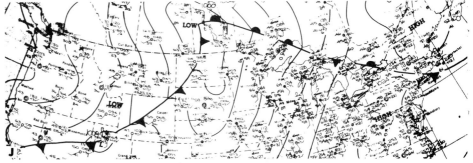

Figure J: Typical of the daily weather map prepared by the National Weather Service, this section shows the position of fronts and highs and lows across the upper United States and Canada. Such maps may be obtained from the Superintendent of Documents, U.S. Government Printing Office, Washington, D.C. 20402. Curved lines joining points where atmospheric pressure is the same are called isobars.

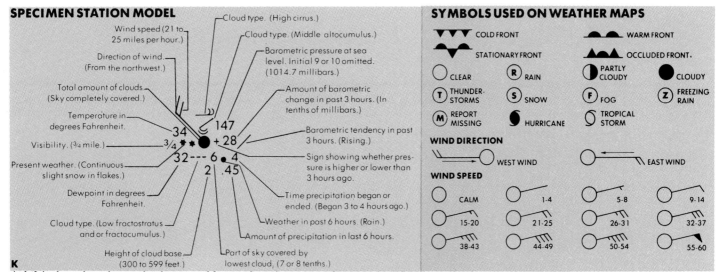

SPECIMEN STATION MODEL

Cloud type. (High cirrus.)

Cloud type. (Middle altocumulus.)

Wind speed (21 to 25 miles per hour.)

Barometric pressure at sea level. Initial 9 or 10 omitted. (1014.7 millibars.)

Direction of wind. (From the northwest.)

Total amount of clouds. (Sky completely covered.)

Amount of barometric change in past 3 hours. (In tenths of millibars.)

Temperature in degrees Fahrenheit.

Barometric tendency in past 3 hours. (Rising.)

Visibility. (¾ mile.)

Sign showing whether pressure is higher or lower than 3 hours ago.

Present weather. (Continuous slight snow in flakes.)

Time precipitation began or ended. (Began 3 to 4 hours ago.)

Dewpoint in degrees Fahrenheit.

Weather in past 6 hours. (Rain.)

Cloud type. (Low fractostratus and or fractocumulus.)

Amount of precipitation in last 6 hours.

Height of cloud base. (300 to 599 feet.)

Part of sky covered by lowest cloud. (7 or 8 tenths.)

SYMBOLS USED ON WEATHER MAPS

COLD FRONT
WARM FRONT
STATIONARY FRONT
OCCLUDED FRONT.
CLEAR
R RAIN
PARTLY CLOUDY
CLOUDY
T THUNDER-STORMS
S SNOW
F FOG
Z FREEZING RAIN
M REPORT MISSING
HURRICANE
TROPICAL STORM

WIND DIRECTION
WEST WIND
EAST WIND

WIND SPEED
CALM
1-4
5-8
9-14
15-20
21-25
26-31
32-37
38-43
44-49
50-54
55-60

At left is shown how the weather is reported from each station on a weather map. At right, what some of the symbols on a weather map mean.

Professional forecasters find it difficult to predict when an intense tropical storm will become a hurricane and which way it will move when it does. Hurricanes tend to form over tropical Atlantic waters during August, September, and October, and, less frequently, in the southwestern Caribbean and the Gulf of Mexico in May, June, and November. They tend to move eastward and northward, and may strike either the Gulf States or the Atlantic Coast. On a weather map, hurricanes will show no fronts but a tightly circular pattern of isobar lines (Figure J, opposite) marking the rapidly falling barometric pressure that is associated with them.

Some Help in Forecasting

With instruments and cloud observations, you can forecast the weather for the next 12 to 24 hours. But how does one forecast the weather for the day after tomorrow, or the day after that? Here you need the help provided by weather maps supplied by the National Weather Service (Figure J). These are reproduced in abridged form in most daily newspapers, together with a chart explaining the symbols used on them (Figure K). These symbols indicate the clouds, wind direction, wind speed, pressure, temperature, humidity, and precipitation at each of a nationwide network of weather observation stations. Since air masses and fronts move generally from west to east in North America, the readings at some of the stations west clue you in on weather to come. But fronts do not move from west to east in a straight line; as Figures L and M show, they are likely to do quite a bit of swooping and swerving. When your instrument readings for temperature, moisture, and wind direction move toward a weather map reading of some weather station to the west of you, this may indicate where you are in relation to the moving fronts and air masses. Even if you don't have a weather map and haven't checked your instruments, if there is a steady wind you can find where you are in relation to the center of oncoming highs and lows. Stand with your back to the wind and the atmospheric pressure will be lower on your left than your right, and lower to the left front than the left rear. This rule, known as Buys Ballot's Law, holds true for the northern hemisphere; its reverse is true for the southern hemisphere.

Don't Be Discouraged

As you begin forecasting, you will find that many of your forecasts will not be accurate. Don't despair. Even professionals, supported by a worldwide network of observers, sophisticated instruments, satellites, and computers that monitor every characteristic of the vast ocean of air above, are right only about 85 percent of the time. The weather is simply too complex and capricious to pinpoint unerringly. If half of your forecasts are right, you will be doing well. And the more you study what happens, the better you will do.

For related projects and entries, see "Maps and Pathfinding" and "Piloting Small Boats."

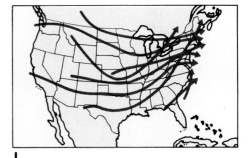

L
Figure L: These are characteristic lines of travel of lows (low pressure areas) across the continental United States.

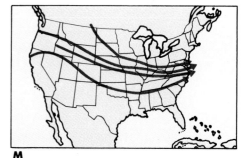

M
Figure M: These are characteristic lines of travel of highs (high pressure areas) across the continental United States.

WEAVING
Over and Under

Weaving has played a role throughout the history of mankind. Remnants of textiles thousands of years old attest to its importance through the ages. Artifacts from ancient civilizations include early looms that were made of twigs on which the lengthwise (warp) threads were tied. To facilitate weaving, in which lengthwise and crosswise threads are interlocked to form a fabric, the lengthwise threads are held taut on a loom while the crosswise threads are passed over and under them. The lengthwise threads as a group are called the warp; crosswise threads together are known as the weft or the filling. Over the centuries, looms have become far more complex than twigs, but whatever kind of loom is used, the purpose is the same: to keep the lengthwise threads under an even tension so the process of interlocking warp and weft is easier.

Four-Harness Loom
The projects that follow were woven on what is called a four-harness loom, shown opposite. This is a loom which speeds the over-and-under process of weaving by raising preselected warp threads. How this is done is described in the Craftnotes on page 2754. The space between the raised warp threads and the others is called a shed. The weaver passes the weft thread, the filling, through a shed, then tamps it snugly into place. This is weaving: lifting a selected set of warp threads, passing the weft through the space created, and beating the weft into position. When a different set of warp threads is lifted, a new shed is created for the weft to pass through, locking the preceding weft thread in place. Before any weaving can be done, however, the work must be planned and the warp put on the loom.

Planning the Warp
The weaver opposite has given much thought to the shawl she is making. Before she started to weave, she determined the color, weight, texture, and fiber content of the yarn; the size of the finished shawl; the density and design of the weave; and the finishing techniques she will use.

   The first step is to determine the size of the product and the weight and texture of yarn to be used. As you gain experience, you learn the properties of various yarns, how they weave, and how much will be needed. Because the warp threads must go over and under the weft threads, an extra allowance called take-up, ranging from 10 to 15 percent, is added to the calculations. The amount of yarn listed for the projects that follow was calculated for the specific yarn used. With a heavier or lighter weight, the amount would change. If a denser fabric is sought, more threads per inch are woven, so the amount of yarn needed increases. When you estimate the amount needed, remember that the heavier a yarn is, the less yardage there is in a skein of a given number of ounces.

Color, Texture, and Design
The interplay of color and texture often comes as a pleasant surprise as the weaving progresses. The texture can be controlled to some extent by the choice of yarn—soft or rough, smooth or nubby, tightly or loosely spun. But color is probably the first thing you will notice in a weaving. When you choose yarn colors, take a strand of each possibility and twist them together. This approximates the way they will look when woven. The amount of any color used affects the result: a weave with two balanced colors will look quite different from the same colors in a weave with one dominant color. Any single color area will look richer if it includes yarns in a range of shades and textures of the one color.

Bev Nerenberg is shown weaving on a four-harness floor loom. Behind her are yarns in a vast array of colors and textures. She finds the yarns useful for design inspiration as well as for the actual weaving. In the foreground of this photograph is the loom's warp beam from which warp threads are fed over the back beam and through the harnesses. At the left is a ratchet that controls the tension of these warp threads; near the floor are the treadles that move the harnesses that maneuver the warp threads to make weaving possible.

Bev Nerenberg studied weaving at the Craft Students' League and at the Fashion Institute of Technology in New York. Then she undertook an intensive study of weaving, finishing, draft analysis, textile materials, and lace making at Väukolonien Säterglänten, a weaving school in Insjön, Sweden. Bev has also experimented with spinning, natural dyeing, tapestry weaving, and pile weaves. She teaches weaving at the Philadelphia College of Art and at her yarn shop in New York, which also stocks looms, weaving and spinning equipment, and instruction books. Items that Bev designs and weaves are sold at department stores and boutiques in New York.

The overall effect of a weaving comes from the combination of color, texture, and patterns formed by warp and weft threads. The spacing of the warp and weft as well as the weight of the yarn affects the weight and feel of the fabric. Repeat areas—of color, of pattern, or of plain weave—add interest to a design. When all elements of the weaving work together, they relate to each other to produce a unified end result.

CRAFTNOTES: THE FOUR-HARNESS LOOM

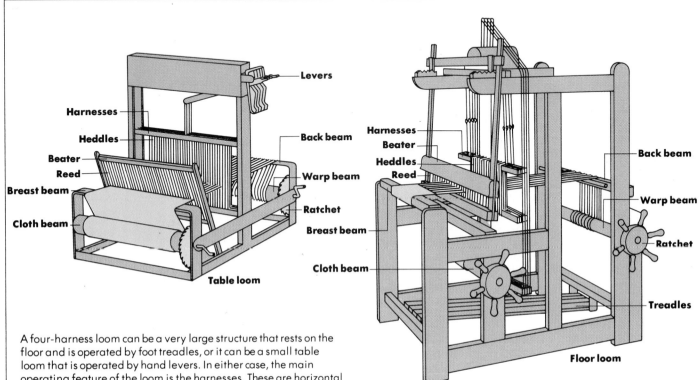

A four-harness loom can be a very large structure that rests on the floor and is operated by foot treadles, or it can be a small table loom that is operated by hand levers. In either case, the main operating feature of the loom is the harnesses. These are horizontal bars of wood to which heddles—lengths of string or metal strips with holes called eyes in them—are attached. When the length-wise warp threads are put on the loom, they are threaded through the heddle eyes and thus attached to the harnesses. When any one harness is moved, the warp threads attached to it are raised, creating a space called a shed for the crosswise weft thread to pass through. This thread automatically goes over some threads (those attached to the harnesses not moved) and under others (those raised with the harness). The threads raised are the ones that show in a given row of weaving; the others are covered by the weft. When another harness is moved, a different set of warp threads is raised, locking the previous row of weaving in place and contributing to the development of the pattern.

How the harnesses are operated depends on the type loom you have. But basically, in a floor loom, harnesses are attached to slats of wood called lams which in turn are attached to treadles (foot pedals). When you press on a treadle with your foot, it pulls down on the lam and moves the harness. A treadle can be attached to more than one lam, so one foot movement can move more than one harness. The pattern of attachment of treadles to lams to harnesses is called the tie-up, which can vary from weave to weave. The mechanics of this attachment varies from loom to loom and is detailed in the manufacturer's instructions.

In a table loom, the harnesses are attached to levers, and each harness is operated independently of the others. If you are working on a weave that calls for harnesses one and three to move simultaneously, you would have to press two levers.

Other features of the two looms are similar. As illustrated above, both have a warp beam on which the warp threads are wound and stored. From the warp beam, the threads go over the back beam, through the heddles on the harnesses, and through the reed—a rectangle with slots in it at intervals to evenly spread the warp threads to the desired weaving width. After the weft thread is passed through the warp, it is pressed tightly against the preceding rows of weft by the beater, a movable part that also serves to hold the reed. The woven fabric passes over the breast beam and is finally wound onto the cloth beam. Ratchets on the warp and cloth beams maintain an even tension on the warp threads.

A loom is often a lifetime investment involving a considerable amount of money. So it pays to investigate the alternatives. One factor is size. Although the amount of space you have may dictate whether you buy a floor or table loom, there is a variety of sizes and weights of looms within either category. The weight of the loom is important if you plan to move it. Size also affects the weaving width because the weaving capacity of a loom is determined by the width of the harnesses. Another factor is the construction of the loom. Some looms are made entirely of wood; others are wood and metal. The placement of the treadles, the way the beater is attached to the loom, and the movement of the harnesses vary with each loom. The best way to decide on a loom is to weave on it. Try as many looms as possible by inquiring at yarn shops, the local Y, adult education courses, or the textile department of a nearby college or university.

Glossary

Back beam: A piece of wood at the back of the loom over which the warp threads travel. The back beam together with the breast beam helps keep the warp threads at an even tension.

Beaming: Winding the warp onto the warp beam under tension.

Beater: A movable part of the loom that, when moved forward, tamps the filling into place. The reed fits into the beater.

Beating: Tamping the weft thread into position.

Breast beam: A piece of wood at the front of the loom. It provides a surface for the woven fabric to travel over as it is wound onto the cloth beam.

Chain: A series of loops, similar to a crochet chain, made with warp for easier handling from the warping board to the loom.

Cloth beam: A piece of wood below the breast beam onto which the woven cloth is wound.

Cross: Warp ends alternately crossing as they pass a peg on a warping board, to simplify loom threading by keeping ends in order and free of tangles.

Dent: The space between the metal pieces in a reed through which warp is threaded. Reeds come in various sizes according to the number of dents per inch.

Draft: A drawing of a weave pattern on graph paper showing the threading and the weaving order.

Dressing the loom: Preparing the loom for weaving; warping the loom.

Ends: Individual lengths of warp threads.

Filling: The yarn used to weave horizontally, also called weft.

Harnesses: Horizontal bars on which the heddles are strung.

Heading: The first few inches woven onto a new warp in plain weave—before the actual weaving begins—to help keep the warp threads evenly spaced.

Heddles: Pieces of metal or string with a center eye through which the warp yarn is threaded.

Lams: Lower levers connecting harnesses and treadles on a floor loom; they allow weaver to move several harnesses with one treadle.

Lease sticks: Thin, flat sticks inserted into the warp on either side of the cross to keep the cross in order while warping the loom.

Lever: A device attached to the harnesses on a table loom. Pressing the lever raises the harness.

Pick-up stick: A thin, flat beveled stick with a pointed end which is used to make an extra shed for pattern weaving.

Ratchets: Wheels with teeth that help maintain an even tension on the warp threads. One ratchet is at the cloth beam, the other at the warp beam.

Reed: A removable metal device that fits in the beater; it has slots called dents that space the warp threads evenly. Reeds are identified by the number of dents per inch.

Reed hook: A tool with a hook at one end that is used to pull warp ends through the dents (spaces) in the reed.

Selvage: The right and left edges of the weaving, paralleling the warp threads.

Shed: The space between warp threads made when a number are raised, permitting the passage of the shuttle carrying weft thread.

Shot: A single passage of the weft or filling thread through a shed.

Shuttle: The tool used to carry the weft or filling thread.

Sleying: Threading the warp through the dents in the reed.

Tabby: The basic weave formed by raising every other warp thread, also called plain weave.

Take-up: The contraction of yarn caused by the interlocking of warp and weft.

Tie-up: The joining of treadles with harnesses of a floor loom, following the pattern draft, so the harnesses can be moved by foot.

Treadles: Foot pedals on a floor loom that are attached to the lams that, in turn, are attached to the harnesses.

Twill: A basic weave in which the warp and weft form diagonal lines.

Warp: The lengthwise threads that are put on the loom, under tension, through which the weft is woven.

Warp beam: A rotating beam below the back beam on which the unwoven warp is wound and stored.

Warping board: A wooden frame with pegs around which warp is measured.

Weft: The yarn used to weave horizontally across the warp, also called filling.

Weft-faced cloth: Cloth in which the weft is beaten down very tightly so it completely conceals the warp.

Weaving, Braiding, and Knotting
Plaid pillow

Fabric woven on a single set of vertical (warp) threads can have a variety of patterns, depending on how the horizontal (weft) threads are used. On the front of this pillow (left), an even plaid was created by weaving gray, black, and brown weft threads through gray, black, and brown warp stripes. The back of the pillow (right), woven on the same warp stripes, has a different pattern because only brown weft thread was used.

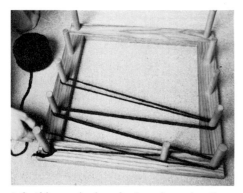

1: On this warping board, a 2-yard warp length was measured from the peg where the yarn is tied (lower left corner) to the third peg on the left. (A 4-yard warp would extend to the last peg on the left.) Each thread warped on this path will be the same length. The cross being formed (bottom center) helps keep the threads in order.

A

Figure A: By wrapping alternate rounds of warp thread on either side of the second peg of the warping board, you form a cross. This helps keep the threads in order. While the warp is still on the board, loosely tie a contrasting color of thread around the warp threads at the cross as shown.

2: When all the warp threads are on the warping board and tied together, start at the end farthest from the cross and begin a chain by forming a loop and pulling the free end of the warp through the loop, making another loop to pull the warp through.

The plaid pillow shown on page 2755, the scarf on page 2765, and the pillow shown on page 2767 were all woven on the same set of vertical warp threads. Putting warp threads on a loom is a time-consuming process, and since the structure of the loom allows a much longer warp than is necessary for any one project, several things are usually woven with one warp. It is possible, of course, to change the pattern with changes in the weft or with a new tie-up.

Determining the Warp

To determine the length of the warp threads that will be put on the loom, first add the length of the finished piece, plus any hems or fringe, plus approximately one yard for loom waste. (Loom waste, the amount of yarn necessary to tie the warp to the loom, varies with each loom, but when you become familiar with a loom, you can make this adjustment accurately.) Add to this 10 to 15 percent for take-up, a combination of the amount of shrinkage you can anticipate when the fabric is released from the tension of the loom and the fact that the threads go over and under each other. For example, the pillow shown is 10¼ inches wide, although its weaving width measured 11¼ inches. The take-up allowance also compensates for shrinkage in finishing. This total—length, hems, take-up allowance, and loom waste—is the length of the warp. The warp length for the first three projects was determined as follows: 24 inches for each of the two pillows, 2 inches for hems on each pillow, 50 inches for the scarf, and 10 inches for its fringe. This total is 112 inches. Adding 10 percent for take-up and 24 inches for loom waste on this loom, the total becomes 148 inches, or approximately 4 yards, so each thread put on the loom was 4 yards long.

To determine how many warp threads you need, you must decide how wide you want the finished pieces to be and how dense the weave, which determine the number of threads per inch. Then multiply these together. The pillows and scarf are 11¼ inches wide on the loom, and there are eight threads per inch, so the total is 90 warp threads. To determine the number of yards of yarn necessary for the warp, multiply the number of threads by the length of the warp. In this case it is 90 times 4, or 360 yards total warp. This calculation is for a specific yarn and weaving density—Peruvian alpaca at eight threads to the inch. If you use a thicker or thinner yarn, or a different density, your total will be different. Most yarn companies will supply information about how many yards there are in a pound of a given yarn so you can figure how many pounds of yarn you need in each color chosen for the warp. For these articles, the warp was to be striped in the following pattern: 12 brown, 2 gray, 10 black, 2 gray, 12 brown, 2 gray, 10 black, 2 gray, 12 brown, 2 gray, 10 black, 2 gray, and 12 brown, making up the total of 90 warp threads. That meant slightly more than half the total was brown, one-third was black, and about one-sixth was gray.

3: As you keep pulling the free end of the warp through, you form successive loops. Continue until the entire warp is one long chain.

4: To straighten warp ends, put a weight on the chained end. (To speed warping, this warp was wound on the warping board with two strands; hence there are pairs of threads going over and under the lease sticks.)

5: To get the warp beamed on the loom (wound onto the warp beam) at the proper width, a hook (called a reed hook) is used to pull the warp ends through slots called dents in a metal frame called a reed.

6: Since this is a preliminary step to get the proper weaving width only (it will be repeated later on the loom), it can be speeded by pulling groups of four threads through every fourth dent.

To estimate the amount of weft or filling thread you need, multiply the weaving width, here 11¼ inches, times the number of weft threads per inch, here eight, times the number of inches to be woven, 26 inches for the first project, the plaid-faced pillow. Then add 10 percent for take-up. This totals 2,574 inches, or 71½ yards of thread.

Preparing the Warp

To prepare the warp for the loom, each thread must be the length needed. To facilitate this, the yarn is first wrapped on a warping board (photograph 1, opposite). This is a wooden frame with pegs that jut out at intervals. The warp yarn is wound and measured on these pegs. First, the length needed is measured on the warping board. In photograph 1, a 2-yard length reaches from the peg at the lower left corner to the peg in the middle of the left side, following the zigzag course pictured. A 4-yard length would extend to the last peg on the left. On the warping board, the second warp thread goes from the upper peg back to the first. So the yarn is wound in the zigzag path and back to the first peg a total of 45 times to get 90 warp threads. By taking alternate paths around the second peg, a cross is formed. The purpose of the cross is to keep the warp threads in order until they are threaded onto the loom. As the warp threads are wound on the warping board, tie on new colors as necessary to achieve the striped warp described above. To count the warp threads, loosely tie a cord around every 30 threads. When you have wound all 90 threads on the warping board, tie the yarn to the last peg and cut off the excess. Then tie contrasting yarn securely around each section—the beginning, the end, and most importantly, the cross (Figure A). These cords help keep the warp threads from tangling until they are put on the loom. Slip the warp loops off the terminal peg; then chain the warp to make it easier to handle. Start at the end farthest from the cross and make a loop with the yarn (photograph 2). Pull the yarn through the loop (photograph 3) to form the next loop. Continue until the entire length of the warp up to the tied cross is chained.

To keep the warp threads in order, insert a thin stick (called a lease stick) in either side of the cross. Tie the sticks loosely to each other, using the holes in the ends. Then untie the cord around the cross and any cords used to help count threads so you can spread out the warp. You can see the order of the warp threads more clearly if you put a weight on the warp threads and pull the threads taut (photograph 4). To spread out the warp to the desired weaving width before putting it on the loom, draw the warp threads through a metal frame with vertical slots called a reed. These reeds come with various numbers of slots (called dents) per inch; choose the reed according to how many threads per inch you want. The reed pictured has eight dents per inch (photograph 5). Use a reed hook, a tool with a hook on one end, to pull the threads through the slots. Since this is only a preliminary step to establish the weaving width (it will be repeated later with the reed on the loom), you can pull four threads through every fourth dent rather than one through each dent (photograph 6). But the threads should be centered in the reed, in this case, extending 5⅝ inches on either side of the reed's center.

7: Here, the reed is being inserted in the beater, the part of the loom that the weaver pulls forward to tamp down the weft. The chained yarn is draped over the front beam.

8: The unchained loops of the warp beyond the reed are then slipped on to the warp apron-stick at the back of the loom.

9: The chained warp is tied to the front beam. This top view shows the warp evenly spaced on the warp apron-stick (top), passing through the reed in the beater (center), and tied to the front beam. The lease sticks are still between the beater and the breast beam.

Warping the Loom

The warp is now ready to be transferred to the loom. One way to beam the warp is to start from the back, the side opposite the weaver. Figure B shows the route the warp threads will take; they are wound onto the warp beam, then threaded from the back to the front. Insert the reed into the beater, with the loops that were pulled through the reed facing the back of the loom (photograph 7). Transfer the looped ends of warp threads to the warp apron-stick (photograph 8). This is a stick that is attached with cord to the warp beam at the back of the loom. Tie the chained end of warp securely to the front beam, and straighten the warp threads on the apron bar so they are spaced as evenly as they are in the reed (photograph 9). Then untie the chained front of the warp so you can wind the warp over the back beam and down to the warp beam (photograph 10). To maintain even tension, it is easier if one person is at the rear of the loom winding on the warp and another person is at the front of the loom keeping the warp flowing smoothly.

Begin winding the warp on the warp beam, placing sticks, paper, or cardboard around the beam during the first round and once each four rounds thereafter (photograph 11). These inserts keep a flat surface to maintain an even tension on the warp threads. When the warp is nearly all on the warp beam, move the lease sticks from the front to the back of the reed. To do this, untie the lease sticks and raise the one nearest the beater; insert a third stick in the space created behind the reed (photograph 12). Remove the stick you raised initially, and raise the other lease stick, moving the first stick to the back of the reed. Replace the third stick with the second lease stick; then tie the lease sticks together again (photograph 13). Slide the lease sticks back and tie them to the back beam. Cut the end loops in front of the reed so you can pull groups of warp threads out and knot them loosely at the back beam (photograph 14). Now the warp can be threaded back to the front of the loom. This time, each warp thread is passed through a heddle, a metal strip or

10: To wind the warp onto the warp beam, take the warp apron-stick over the back beam and down to the warp beam. Place a stick on each of the flat sides of the warp beam to keep an even tension on the threads.

11: After the warp is wound around the warp beam once, a thin stick is placed on the warp beam every fourth round until all the warp is on the warp beam. These sticks help maintain an even tension on the threads.

12: Next the lease sticks are moved behind the beater. Raise one stick and insert a third stick temporarily in the space thus created between the warp threads behind the beater.

13: Raise the second lease stick; then slip out the first and move it behind the beater the same way. Replace the temporary stick with the second lease stick, and tie the sticks together again.

14: Here, the lease sticks are tied to the back beam, and the warp threads, the looped ends cut, are pulled through from the front of the loom, and knotted loosely together in groups.

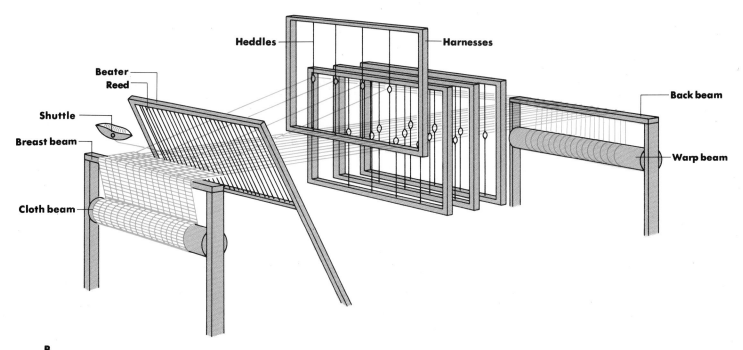

B
Figure B: This drawing shows the path taken by the warp threads through the loom, from the unwoven warp threads stored on the warp beam at the back of the loom to the woven cloth wound onto the cloth beam at the front of the loom.

15: Thread individual warp threads from the back of the loom through the eyes in the heddles which are attached to each of the harnesses. Loosely knot groups of threads.

16: After all the warp threads are threaded through the heddles, each thread must be taken through a slot—called a dent—in the reed to get the proper weaving width.

17: Use a reed hook to take each thread through each dent in the reed. Loosely knot clusters of warp threads together in front of the reed to keep any from slipping out.

string with an eye in the center. The heddles are attached to the harnesses—movable sections that move the warp threads up and down. Count the number of heddles needed; here it is 90, one for each warp thread. Push the others out of the way. Then thread the warp threads through the heddles in sequence (photograph 15). Make sure you take the threads through in the order from the cross. The order of threading used here is called a straight draw or simply 1-2-3-4. This means the first thread, starting at the right side, is drawn through a heddle on the first harness, the second through a heddle on the second harness, the third through the third harness, the fourth through the fourth harness, the fifth through the first harness, and so on. This 1-2-3-4 pattern is repeated until all the warp threads are threaded through the heddles. As eight or ten threads are threaded, knot them together loosely in front of the heddles so they do not slip out. Check often to make sure the 1-2-3-4 pattern is maintained. When you have taken all the threads through the heddles, find the center of the reed and measure the width of the warp so it is evenly spaced on either side. Using the reed hook, pull the warp threads through the spaces (dents) in the reed, being careful to take them in the order they were put through the heddles (photograph 16). This time, draw one warp thread

18: Tie the warp threads to the front apron-stick. To keep the stick parallel with the front beam, tie the center cluster of threads first, then follow with each end cluster.

19: Then tie each of the clusters of warp threads between the end clusters to the front apron-stick, using an overhand knot as shown. These knots will be adjusted before they are tied again.

20: Adjust the knots until the front apron-stick is again parallel with the front beam. Then tie each of the knots again to secure them.

through each space (photograph 17). Loosely knot clusters of threads in front of the reed so they do not accidentally pull out. Check the threading often to make sure you have not missed a slot or pulled two threads through one space.

Now tie the warp to the front apron-stick which is attached to the cloth beam on which the woven fabric will be wound. Tie the middle cluster of threads from in front of the reed to the apron stick; then tie each end cluster (photograph 18). Take each cluster of threads over the top of the apron stick and around to the back of it. Divide the group in half and tie with an overhand knot on top of the threads. Adjust these three knots until the apron stick is parallel to the front beam. Continue tying other groups of threads (photograph 19). Pull each knot tight. Check the tension of the threads by running your hand over them. When the tension feels equal, tie each of the knots again at each point to secure the threads so they will not come loose while they are being woven (photograph 20). The warp is now on the loom and ready to be woven. With a table loom, the preparatory work is finished. With a floor loom, you still must tie up the foot treadles to the harnesses. Following the loom manufacturer's instructions, attach harnesses one and three to the first treadle and harnesses two and four to the second treadle.

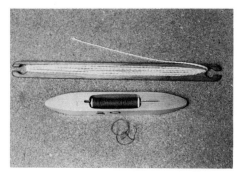

21: The weft thread can be wrapped around a stick shuttle (top) or wound onto a bobbin that is inserted into a boat shuttle (bottom).

22: To weave, use the treadle to move the harnesses so you create a space, called a shed, between sets of warp threads. Pass the shuttle carrying the weft thread through this shed from side to side.

23: To close the spaces between the warp threads where they are tied to the front apron-stick, a woven heading is needed. You can make this by weaving 1 to 2 inches, changing the shed with each change of direction, without tamping down the weft with the beater.

The Filling

To prepare the filling (weft) for weaving, wind it onto a shuttle, the tool you will use to carry the weft through the warp threads. There are various kinds of shuttles (photograph 21); the kind you use will depend on the size of your loom and the type of yarn used. A stick shuttle is a flat wooden stick with a cutout at either end. Yarn is wound around the shuttle so it fits inside the cutouts. A boat shuttle is a wood frame with a steel pin that holds a removable bobbin. Yarn is wound onto the bobbin which is then slipped onto the shuttle. Several bobbins of one color, or one bobbin in each color being used, can be wound in advance and placed on the shuttle as needed, speeding the weaving process.

Weaving

You are now ready to weave. Although warping the loom is time-consuming and requires patience, you will appreciate a well-dressed loom when you start to weave. Warp threads that are on the loom evenly spaced and under even tension make the process of weaving enjoyable and produce fabric that is well made.

To begin weaving the pillow fabric, open a shed—the space between warp threads—by pressing a treadle or lever, depending on the kind of loom you have. Pass the shuttle through this shed from one side to the other, slipping the end of the weft thread around the end warp thread and back into the same shed (photograph 22). Since the warp is tied into groups at the front apron-stick, there are spaces between the clusters. To close these spaces so the warp threads are as evenly spaced at the point of weaving as they are at the reed, a 1- to 2-inch heading is woven. One way to do this is to use string or heavy yarn to weave back and forth, changing the shed with each change of direction and beating down the weft with the beater after each pass of the shuttle. Another way is to weave back and forth two or three times with weft thread, without beating down and then beat them all together (photograph 23). When you reach the point where the warp threads are evenly spaced, you are ready to begin the regular weaving. Open a shed with the treadle or lever, and pass the shuttle through this opening so the weft thread lies loosely in the warp. This lets the weft thread go over and under the warp threads without pulling them together tightly. Tamp this weft snugly into place by pulling the beater forward, then letting it go back to its original position. The harder you beat down each weft thread, the more tightly packed the weft will be. How hard you want to beat depends on the yarn you are using and what you are making.

This is the process of weaving: open the shed, pass the weft through, and beat down, then change the shed, pass the weft through, and beat down. This plain weave—over one warp thread, then under one warp thread—is also called tabby. As the weaving progresses, maintain an even selvage edge. The selvage is formed by the loops of weft thread that you make around the end warp threads at both sides of the fabric. To keep this even, do not let the weft thread extend beyond the end warp, but do not pull it so tight that it pulls in the end warp. An even selvage edge is shown in photograph 24.

To change colors in the weft, start the new color of yarn the same way you began the weft. After passing the weft through the shed, bring the tail of the new color around the end warp thread and back into the same shed (photograph 24). The preceding color was ended the same way, but make sure you start the new color at the side opposite from where you ended the old color to avoid a build up of yarn on one side. Continue weaving until the shed becomes too small to pass the shuttle through. Then release the ratchets on the warp beam and the cloth beam, and wind the woven piece onto the cloth beam, bringing more unwoven warp forward. Tighten the warp and continue weaving.

An Even Plaid

The pillow cover shown on page 2755 is an even plaid. To weave an even plaid, one with warp and weft the same colors and the same pattern repeat, measure the area rather than count the threads. For example, the width of each set of brown warp threads on this pillow is 1½ inches. After the heading (the same brown weft thread), weave a total of 1½ inches of brown. Then weave the gray, following it with black in the same pattern as the warp (photograph 25). Continue weaving until the amount of weft equals the width of the warp. For example, there are four sets of brown threads in the warp, so you need four sets of brown threads in the weft to get the pillow front. Then weave what will become the pillow back, using only brown yarn to emphasize the striped warp.

This completes the weaving of the pillow cover, but do not take it off the loom until you have finished weaving the rest of the warp for the companion projects. Several more pillow covers could be woven on this length of warp, or you can make the scarf and pillow described on the following pages. If a fringe is desired for the next project, loosen the ratchets and wind the woven piece onto the cloth beam so there are unwoven warp threads between projects. When all weaving is completed, cut the project off the loom.

When the weaving is off the loom, it needs to be washed. For any wool fabric, use a mild soap and lukewarm water. If you want the weave to become tighter, shrink it slightly by using hot water and washing vigorously. Roll the fabric in a towel to blot out excess water and lay it flat to dry. When dry, shape it by pressing lightly with a steam iron. To achieve a fuzzy look, as on a scarf for example, brush the woven piece with a hairbrush.

To make the pillow, fold the woven fabric in half lengthwise with right sides facing (Figure C). Stitch around the three open sides with an overcast stitch, using weft yarn, and leave a 5-inch opening on one edge. Turn the pillow right side out and stuff it with loose polyester fiber; then stitch the opening closed by hand. The pillow is not quite square because weaving tends to pull in more in width than in length and because there are two side seams but only one end seam.

24: To start a new color, wrap the end of the weft thread around the end warp thread, and tuck it back in the same shed. When the weft has been beaten in, any end of the weft that shows can be clipped close to the surface of the fabric.

25: To weave an even plaid, measure the width of the warp in each color, and weave the same amount of weft in that color.

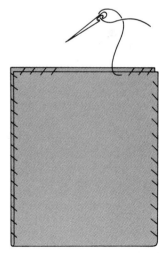

C
Figure C: To make a pillow cover, fold the woven rectangle in half, with right sides facing, and stitch along the three open sides with an overcast stitch, using a piece of warp thread. Leave a 5-inch opening so you can turn the cover right side out, and stuff it with polyester fiber; then stitch the opening closed.

The more harnesses a loom has, the more complicated is its workings. The scarves shown above were woven on an eight-harness loom on the same black and gray striped warp. One scarf has a white weft; the others have black and gray weft. Looms can have eight, twelve, sixteen, or more harnesses.

CRAFTNOTES: PATTERN DRAFTS

A weave is a pattern in woven cloth created by the interaction of warp and weft threads. To duplicate a pattern weave, you use a specific notation known as a pattern draft. This draft is worked on graph paper. It consists of four parts. The draw down is a diagram of how the weave will look, with black squares representing visible warp threads and white squares representing visible weft threads. In order to make this drawing, especially with more complex weaves, however, other information is needed: the threading draft, which shows how the warp threads are put through heddles in the various harnesses; the tie-up draft, which indicates how you tie the harnesses to the treadles so they are lifted together; and the treadling draft, which shows the order in which you push on the treadles.

For the tabby weave, the various drafts would appear as follows:

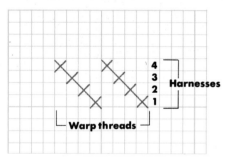

Threading draft
In a threading draft, the horizontal rows represent the harnesses and the vertical rows represent the warp threads. An X means a warp thread should be threaded through the heddle on that harness. If you drafted the entire weaving, there would be the same number of Xs as there are warp threads. But usually two repeats are enough to make the pattern apparent. (The threading pattern shown here is called a straight draw.) The threading order is indicated from right to left.

Tie-up and treadling drafts
For the tie-up in this weave, only two treadles are needed. One treadle is tied to the first and third harnesses; the other to the second and fourth harnesses. (This is a mechanical advantage of the floor loom; with a table loom, the weaver would have to push by hand the levers on the first and third harnesses to make one shed, then the levers for the second and fourth harnesses

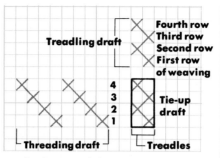

to make the second shed.) In the tie-up draft for the tabby weave, (above, bottom right), the horizontal rows again represent the harnesses, but the vertical rows represent the treadles.

The treadling draft (above, top right) shows the order in which the treadles are pushed. For a tabby weave, the first treadle is pushed, then the second, then the first, then the second, and so on. Again, two repeats are sufficient for the pattern to become apparent.

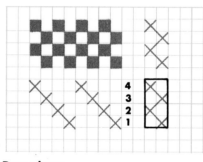

Draw down
From this information, the draw down—the diagram of the weaving—can be made. For the first row of weaving, the X on the treadling draft shows that the first treadle is pushed. According to the tie-up draft, the first treadle lifts the first and third harnesses. The threading draft shows which warp threads are threaded through the first and third harnesses, so those squares on the row representing the first row of weaving are filled in. (A black square represents a raised warp thread.) The second row is drawn the same way. These two rows complete the pattern; the next two rows form a repeat. Since a tabby weave is a simple over-one-under-one weave, the drawing shows the weft (white squares) going over, then under the warp threads (black squares).

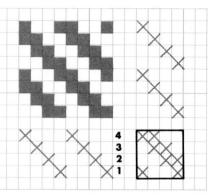

2/2 twill

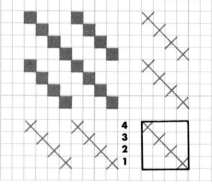

1/3 twill

Twill weaves have a diagonal line formed in the weave. Twills are designated by the number of harnesses up over the number of harnesses down, so a balanced four-harness twill is a 2/2. The surface of this weave has as many warp threads showing as weft threads. Also possible are 1/3 and 3/1 twills; the first has one warp thread showing for every three weft threads, the second has three warp threads showing for every weft thread. Pattern drafts for two of these are shown above.

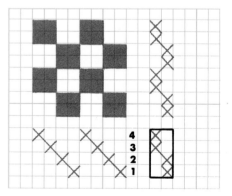

A basket-weave pattern has two weft threads going over two warp threads and under two warp threads; its pattern draft is shown above.

A scarf woven of soft alpaca yarn has vertical stripes, a 5-inch fringe at either end, and lacy bands of openwork called leno.

Weaving, Braiding, and Knotting
Scarf with leno weave

The scarf shown above was woven with the same warp as the pillow described on pages 2755 through 2763. The entire scarf has a striped warp, but the filling is brown except for 1¼-inch bands of black woven at either end. On both sides of each black band are areas of lacy leno—openwork that can be created by manipulating the warp threads. The leno in this scarf has two threads twisted over two adjacent threads. Leno can also be worked with one thread twisted over one adjacent thread, or three threads twisted over the three adjacent threads. You can experiment to see which kind of openwork you prefer. The only additional tool you will need is a pick-up stick, a thin, flat stick with one pointed end; it is used to make an additional shed when you want to create patterns in the weave.

If you weave the scarf after you make the pillow cover previously described, leave about 5 inches of warp threads between the projects to provide a fringe for the scarf. But if this is the first project you weave, the yarn tied to the front apron-stick can become the fringe. Before any lace-making technique is attempted, a

26: To finish the fringe on the scarf, place a book or other weight on the scarf and knot sets of warp threads together with overhand knots. This secures the ends so the weaving will not unravel. Then trim the fringe evenly.

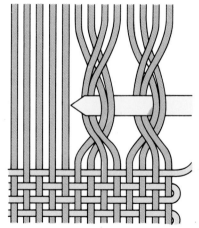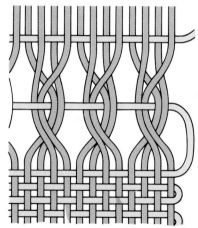

D

Figure D: To maneuver the warp threads to make leno openwork, first close the shed so all the warp threads are at one level. Starting at the right with a pick-up stick, take the two end threads to the left over the next two threads. Then pick up the second pair and slip it on the pick-up stick (left). Continue this way across the warp. Then turn the pick-up stick on its side to create a shed, and put the weft through this shed, as shown at the right. Beat the weft into place with the pick-up stick.

E

Figure E: To keep the ends of the scarf from unraveling, knot each cluster of three fringe threads with an overhand knot as shown.

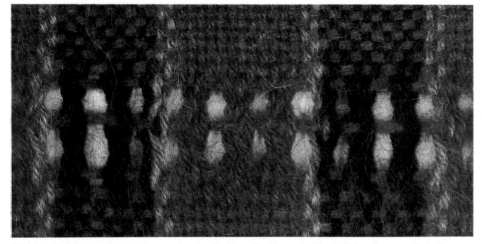

This detail of the scarf shows the openwork called leno that is created by twisting the warp threads.

section of plain weave is needed. This forms a foundation for the openwork. This scarf has 5 inches of plain weave at the beginning. To start the leno, end the section of plain weave with the weft going from left to right. Beat in the weft thread, and close the shed so all four harnesses are at the same level and there is no shed between the warp threads. Put the weft shuttle aside. Starting at the right side, with your fingers pull the first two right-hand threads to the left over the next two threads. Then, using the pointed end of the stick, pick up the second two threads on the stick and let the first two threads fall under the stick, creating a twist (Figure D). With these two threads still on the stick, pull threads five and six to the left over threads seven and eight. Pick up threads seven and eight on the stick. Continue this way across the piece, each time picking up the two threads that are up after the twist is made. When you finish the row, half of the warp threads will be on the pick-up stick. Turn the flat stick on edge to create a space for the weft. Put the weft through from right to left. Turn the stick flat again and use it to push the weft thread against the twists in the warp threads. Remove the stick and make a shed with the treadle or lever. This causes the threads to twist again. Add a row of weft from left to right and beat it down, checking to make sure the spaces formed by the twists are even. Then you can work another row of leno or continue weaving the tabby. The scarf shown has 2 inches of tabby in the brown weft, then 1¼ inches of black, 2 inches of brown, and another row of leno. The body of the scarf is 21 inches of tabby weave in brown; then the same pattern of leno and black band is repeated on the opposite end.

If you are going to continue weaving with the same warp, leave 5 inches of warp threads unwoven before you start the next project. These will become the fringe for the scarf. When you cut the scarf off the loom, cut it 5 inches from the weaving. Then lay it flat and place a book or other weight on it (photograph 26) as you knot groups of warp threads with overhand knots (Figure E). When you have knotted all the warp threads, trim the ends of the fringe evenly; then wash and brush the scarf as directed on page 2763.

Weaving, Braiding, and Knotting
Twill pillow

This pillow was woven on the same warp used to make the pillow on page 2755, but it has a completely different look because it was woven in a twill pattern, producing the visible diagonal lines.

The third project worked with the original striped warp (page 2756) is the twill pillow above. A twill weave is one in which the warp threads appear as diagonal lines, due to the order and combination of the harnesses used (see Craftnotes, page 2764). The pillow is 10¼ by 12 inches and requires the same amount of weft, 71½ yards, as the plaid pillow. The weft is Peruvian alpaca, mostly beige but with three stripes of brown inserted at random.

The weaving process for twill or any other patterned weave is the same as for tabby weave: you open a shed, pass the weft through, beat down, change the shed, pass the weft through, beat down. What makes the twill design appear is the order in which the harnesses are raised. For a balanced twill, one that has as many warp threads as weft threads showing, raise the harnesses in the following sequence: the first and second harnesses, then the second and third, then the third and fourth, and finally the fourth and first. In a floor loom, the harnesses are tied to the treadles to produce this sequence. With a table loom, the weaver must push levers in this order. A twill can be woven on any four-harness loom.

To cover the pillow, a 26-inch length of fabric was woven. If this ends the warp threads on the loom, the pillow can be cut off the loom. If not, you can continue weaving the next project, taking the pillow cover off the loom only when all the weaving is finished. When the pillow cover is cut off the loom, wash it as directed on page 2763.

To make the pillow, follow the instructions on page 2763.

Smart-looking woven jackets can be made by stitching together handwoven rectangles.

Weaving, Braiding, and Knotting
Twill jackets

The three jackets shown above were woven on one warp, but each has a different weft or filling thread. Each jacket is simply constructed of two long panels, each 9¼ by 44 inches (plus a 4-inch fringe at each end). These are sewn together as shown in Figure F. The longer sleeves on one jacket are made by adding a 9¼-by-16-inch woven piece to each armhole.

The total warp yarn needed for all three jackets is 1 pound 10 ounces of 2-ply pure Swedish wool. To weave only one jacket, you will need approximately 10 ounces of yarn for the warp. You also need a reed with 15 dents per inch to get a dense, close weave. The first ten warp threads and the last ten are orange; the remainder are dark brown. These orange threads emphasize the selvage edges of each piece, outlining the boxy shape of the finished jackets.

The weft for the jacket with long sleeves is Swedish yarn that is 50 percent wool and 50 percent alpaca in a shade of orange. A total of 12 ounces is needed; seven for the vest and five for the sleeves. The weft needed for the dark brown jacket is seven ounces of pure wool, lightweight Irish Donegal tweed. The third jacket requires nine ounces of pure wool, heavyweight Irish Donegal tweed. The photograph opposite, top, shows the yarns on top of the fabrics that were produced by weaving the yarns together. Using one warp, you can produce very different fabrics by varying the weft thread.

To estimate what size panels you should make, measure your chest or hips (whichever is larger) and add several inches for an easy fit. Divide this measurement by four, since four panels will be sewn together to fit around the body, allowing ¼ inch for stitching the panels together. The jackets are intended to be worn loose; so be generous with your estimates. The finished width will be about 10 percent less than the weaving width, so to make panels 9¼ inches wide, you have to start with a warp 10¼ inches wide. If you want a longer or shorter jacket, add or subtract that amount to one end of the weaving.

The jackets were all woven on one warp—the brown and orange yarn at the top. Each of the three yarns used for the weft are shown at the bottom, resting on the woven fabric they produced.

To make each piece, warp the loom; then leave 4 inches of unwoven warp for the fringe. Weave 44 inches in a twill design (page 2764). Again, leave 4 inches for fringe on that piece and another 4 inches for fringe on the next piece, and weave another 44-inch length. Leave 4 inches for fringe. To make the sleeves, weave two 16-inch lengths. If you prefer you can weave a total of 32 inches, and then, with the weaving off the loom, machine stitch two rows of stitching across the center to prevent unraveling before cutting the piece in half.

To make a jacket, stitch the woven pieces together, as shown in Figure F (left), using orange warp thread with cross stitch. These stitches show, becoming part of the design of the jacket. To make a sleeve, stitch a 16-inch length into a cylinder, and stitch this into the jacket armhole (Figure F, right).

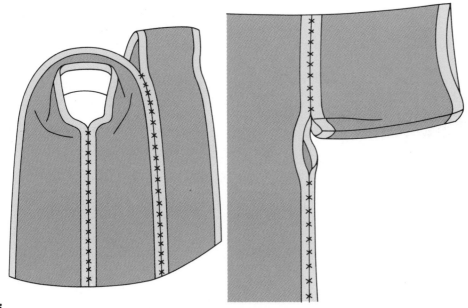

F
Figure F: To make a jacket, stitch the long woven pieces together at the back seam. Then stitch the side seams starting 8 inches down from the shoulder line (left). For sleeves, stitch the 9¼-by-16-inch rectangle into a tube; then stitch the tube to the armhole (right). Do not stitch all the way into the corner; leave about 1½ inches open as shown.

Weft-faced tote bag

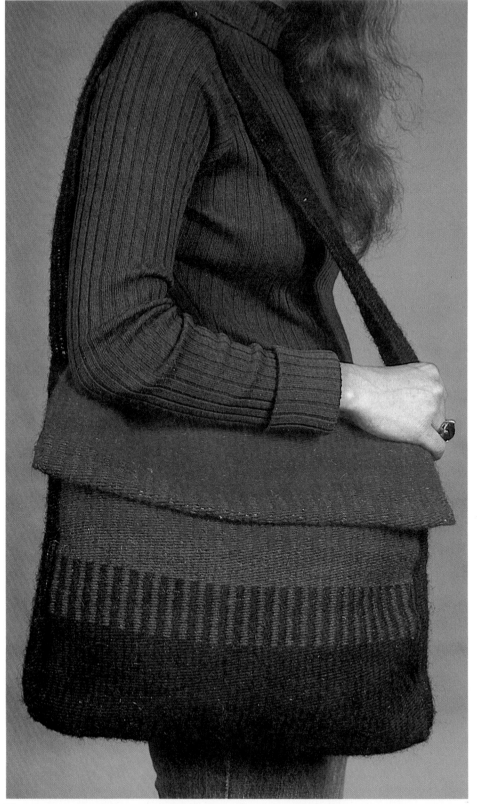

The tricolor design of this roomy tote bag is a result of careful planning before the weaving was begun.

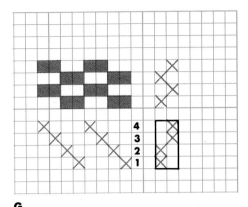

G

Figure G: The pattern draft for the tote bag is shown above (see Craftnotes, page 2764). When the weft is beaten down firmly, the weft threads lie so close to each other that they completely conceal the warp threads.

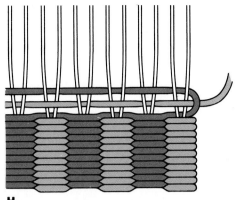

H

Figure H: The heavier weft threads lie next to each other when beaten in so they cover the lightweight warp in a weft-faced weave. Vertical stripes are made by alternating two colors in the weft as shown above.

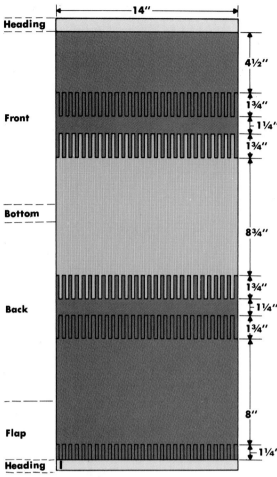

Figure I: The pattern in a weft-faced weave is created by the choice of color used in the weft. The color changes that were required to create the pattern in the tote bag are shown above.

The tote bag shown opposite is a weft-faced weave, that is, a weave in which only the weft threads show on the surface. The three colors you see in the bag, brick, mauve, and navy blue, are all weft thread. To achieve such a weft-faced weave, there are three requirements. The first is that the warp be considerably lighter in weight than the weft. The warp used here is Swedish linen; the weft is a 1-ply Swedish rug yarn that is 75 percent wool and 25 percent goat hair. The second component in a weft-faced weave is that the warp threads are spaced farther apart than they would be if the warp were to show. And the third essential is that the weft is beaten down firmly so each weft thread lies next to the adjacent weft thread with no warp showing between them.

This tote bag required two ounces of warp and one pound of weft to make the 14-by-32-inch rectangle that is folded into an envelope-style bag, as well as the 2-by-54-inch band in the strap and gusset. The warp is threaded onto the loom in a straight draw or 1-2-3-4 sequence (Figure G and Craftnotes, page 2764). The harness tie-up is like that of a basket-weave pattern, with the first and second harnesses tied to one treadle and the third and fourth harnesses tied to another. The treadling order is first, then second, then first, then second. As each weft thread is beaten down firmly, it fills in against the previous weft thread, so together the weft threads conceal all the warp threads. To make a vertical stripe in a weft-faced weave, two weft colors are woven alternately (Figure H). By alternating colors, one will always be on top of a given pair of warp threads, while the other is under those warp threads but on top of the adjacent pair, thus creating vertical stripes when the weft is tamped in place.

Creating a Design

To achieve a specific design in the weave, designing must be done before any yarn is on the loom. The tote-bag design alternates blocks of solid color with blocks of vertical stripes (Figure I). The mauve stripes and solid areas are repeated on both the front and back of the bag in the same place. The front flap also has mauve stripes, so when the flap is closed, the design is continuous from the front of the bag onto the flap. The construction of the bag was planned in advance. The 14-by-32-inch woven rectangle folds into a 12-by-13½-inch envelope purse. This permitted the pattern of the weave to be placed accurately on the rectangle. Careful measuring during the weaving ensured that the designs on the front and back would meet at the sides when the bag was folded, and the design on the flap would match the design on the front of the bag.

To finish both the beginning and ending of the woven panel, a heading of linen was woven with the same linen used in the warp. When the rectangle was removed from the loom, these linen ends were folded under and stitched to the wrong side of the weaving. Then the rectangle was folded and the sides were stitched to the gusset along 12 inches on either end of the 54-inch band, leaving the middle section free to serve as the shoulder strap (Figure J).

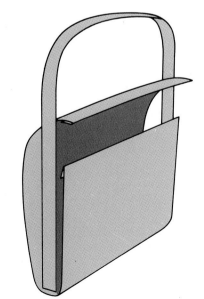

J

Figure J: To make an envelope-style tote bag, fold the back to the front, with the right sides facing in, and stitch the handle to the sides. Then turn the bag right side out.

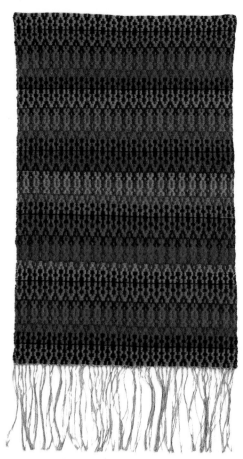

This wall hanging was made by combining three weave patterns and seven colors of weft thread—four for the motifs and three for the background.

Wall hanging

Many intricate designs are possible in weavings made with a four-harness loom. The 20-by-32-inch wall hanging shown at left was made on such a loom. Any particular design is determined by two factors: the order in which the warp threads are threaded through the harnesses, and the order and combination of the harnesses raised to make varying sheds. For this wall hanging, the warp was threaded

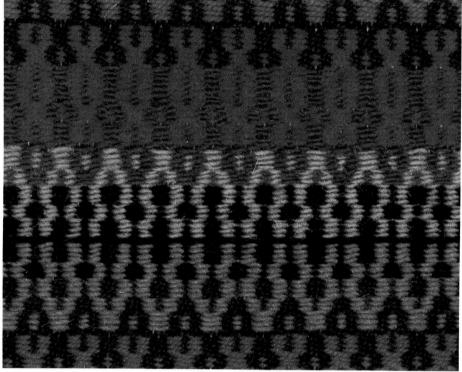

27: The three motifs in the pattern weave for the wall hanging are shown here. They are, starting at the bottom, an urn shape, a mirror image of the urn shape, and a decorative oval.

K

Figure K: Shown at right is the pattern draft for the wall hanging. The colors of the weft threads are listed on the left side; the white squares represent warp threads that will be covered in this weft-faced weave. The three motifs are repeated for the length of the hanging; but the colors of weft are changed. When the first motif is repeated, the seventh color (peach) is used. Then each of the colors is repeated, so there are 12 motifs worked before there is a repeat of the same motif in the same color.

Color key

y	yellow	t	tan
b	brown	o	orange
f	flame	s	sienna

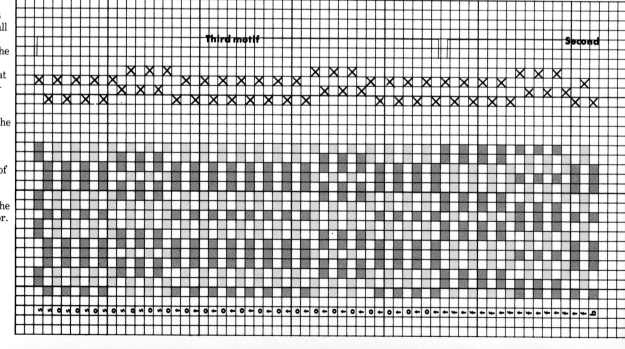

in a pattern known as rosepath on opposites, which is threaded through the harnesses in this order: 1-2-3-4-3-2-1-4. The combination and order of the harnesses raised is indicated in the pattern draft (Figure K). This design consists of three motifs that are repeated for the length of the wall hanging. They are, from top to bottom, an urn shape, a mirror image of the urn shape, and a decorative oval (photograph 27).

To make this wall hanging, 3 ounces of pure Swedish linen was used for the warp, and a total of one pound of pure wool (2-ply Swedish rya rug yarn) in seven colors was used for the weft. Approximately equal amounts of each weft color were used.

The wall hanging is worked in a weft-faced weave, a weave in which only the weft threads show on the surface (page 2771). So all seven colors that show on the surface are colors of weft yarn. In a weft-faced weave, two colors of yarn can be alternated to emphasize the pattern in the weave. In any given area of the wall hanging, one color of yarn forms the motif and another color fills in the background. The seven colors of weft yarn are divided into two groups, one of pattern colors, the other of background colors. The pattern colors used here are yellow, flame, orange, and peach; the background colors are brown, tan, and sienna. The choice of related colors adds to the subtlety of this design.

Since there are three motifs worked in four colors, 12 motifs are worked before there is a repeat of the same motif in the same color. Also the background color is changed in the middle of the motif, giving the effect that the background colors flow into each other. To do this, the first background color was used for the first one and one-half motifs. Then the second background color and each one thereafter were worked for approximately the length of one motif, but starting in the middle of one motif and ending in the middle of the next. This gives each motif two different background colors.

To start this wall hanging, linen warp was put on the loom. A 10-dent reed was used so the warp threads were widely spaced, allowing the weft to be beaten down firmly. A ½-inch heading was woven, using the linen thread as the weft. Then the pattern was begun with the rug yarns. At the end of the weaving, several more rows were woven with the linen thread.

To finish the wall hanging after it was taken off the loom, the heading and the warp ends at the top were stitched to the wrong side. Two groups of warp threads at either side of the top were knotted together to make loops for hanging. At the bottom of the wall hanging, groups of three warp threads were knotted together to make the fringe.

For related entries, see "Inkle Weaving," "Rya and Flossa," "Tablet and Frame Weaving," and "Woven Tapestries."

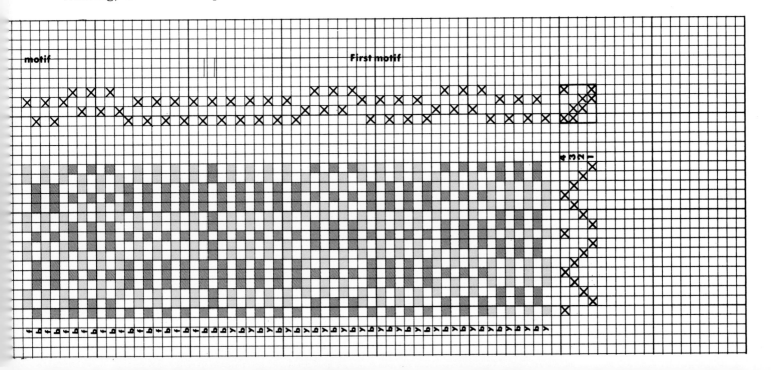

WHISTLES AND FLUTES
Piping On the Wind

Garett Alden grew up in southeast Missouri in an Ozark village of 500 people, where handmade things were still commonplace. When he was about ten, his father taught him how to use hand tools and a wood lathe. He first made a flute on that lathe ten years later. Since then, he has earned a living selling instruments at the Renaissance Pleasure Faires and the Dickens' Fair, among the largest craft fairs on the West Coast. He lives in Mendocino County in northern California.

Flute players were frequently depicted in the art of the ancient Chinese and Egyptians. In these cultures, the flute was a sacred object, used only in rituals and often hidden from the view of women and other uninitiated persons. Whistles, too, were considered things of magic and enchantment by ancient people because they could be used to imitate the sounds of nature. A hunter would often ask a seer or medicine man to make him a whistle he could use to attract a particular kind of game, much the way a modern hunter calls ducks and geese. The magician would summon the spirit of the animal and coax it into the whistle, which he would then plug to keep the spirit inside. Such an aid was believed to ensure the success of the hunt.

While court musicians and priests were playing ritual music, peasants and shepherds were playing simple cane flutes and pipes for their own enjoyment. Gradually, the whistle became largely a child's toy, though it is still used today as a signaling or calling device by police, doormen, hunters, and bird watchers.

Flute music evolved along the two paths. Sacred music developed classical forms; the music of peasants and shepherds became ethnic or folk music.

If you have never played an instrument, the flute is a good place to start. The construction is basic and simple—just a hollow tube with holes. It is played by expelling the breath into or across the blowhole while modulating the tone to create a melody by covering and uncovering other holes with the fingers. When it is mastered, the flute has tones of unsurpassed beauty.

A fifteenth century German woodcut depicts a scene both bucolic and melodic: shepherds at rest with their flocks and their flutes.

These wooden flutes exemplify the art of instrument making. Each was shaped from a rough block of hardwood on a lathe by Garett Alden's practiced hand. The large, two-part flute of baroque design is finished with ivory and brass and sculptural detailing. The small renaissance flutes are of simpler construction.

Opposite: At home with his family in the hills of northern California, Garett Alden delights his daughter Alannah with a melody played on one of his handmade wooden flutes. Although making this type of instrument requires woodworking skill and the use of a wood lathe, Garett described simple alternative methods and materials for making whistles and flutes on pages 2776 through 2779.

Toys and Games
One-tone dowel whistle $ ● ⚭ 🛠

Many a youngster first learned to make a whistle by holding a blade of grass between the first joints of his thumbs and blowing hard into cupped hands. As the blade vibrated and split the airstream, it produced a harsh squawk. The note sounded could be varied by changing the space between the thumbs or using different blades of grass. This principle of the split airstream is basic in whistle making. Whistles can take many forms as long as they incorporate two essential elements—a windway or blowhole and a notch to split the airstream. The most common type of whistle is a short tube blown into from one end.

To make the body of a simple one-tone whistle (below, top), start with a piece of ¾-inch dowel that is 3 or 4 inches long. Dowel is not essential; the shape can be whittled from any suitable scrap of wood. You also need a short length of ⅜-inch dowel, which also could be whittled from scrap. The tools and materials needed are shown in photograph 1; in addition, you need a saw, a ruler and pencil, and a vise or clamp to hold the wood.

After you saw the larger dowel to length, locate the center of one end by measuring and marking a pair of the widest diameters with a ruler and pencil. This is the end that will be drilled to hollow the whistle body. Secure the marked dowel in a vise or clamp with the marked center facing you. Using a ⅜-inch bit, drill 2 inches into the center of the dowel (photograph 2). With the dowel still clamped in the

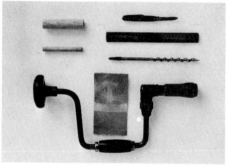

1: These tools and materials are used in making a dowel whistle. At bottom is a brace. Above it are sandpaper; a ⅜-inch auger bit; a half-round coarse and medium file; a pocketknife; and two 4-inch pieces of dowel, ⅜ and ¾ inch in diameter.

2: Clamp the ¾-inch dowel in a vise and drill 2 inches into one end, using a brace and ⅜-inch bit. Keep your arms steady as you drill.

3: File a notch deep enough to cut ⅛ inch into the bored hole, ½ inch in from the mouth end of the whistle. Use the flat side of the file.

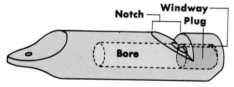

A
Figure A: This drawing of a completed dowel whistle shows the bore, the notch, the plug in position, and the windway.

Notch   Windway   Plug   Bore

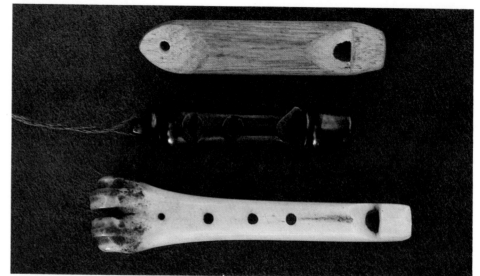

Whistles of dowel, hardwood, and bone seem very different but are, in fact, of similar construction. With any of them, slight alterations in the size of the blowhole would create substantial differences in tone. Whistles are often used by woodsmen to imitate animal and bird sounds.

vise, use the flat side of a medium file or wood rasp to make a notch at an angle to, and ½ inch from, the drilled end (Figure A and photograph 3). The notch should cut into the bored hole about ⅛ inch.

The Windway and Plug

Using the smallest blade of a pocketknife, lightly scrape the top side of the bore in the windway between the open end and the edge of the notch (photograph 4). This will make the bore hole slightly elliptical. Next, make a plug by sawing a piece of ⅜-inch dowel slightly more than ½ inch long. Sand one side of this plug to flatten it a bit (photograph 5), but do not slope the flattened edge. Slide the plug into the windway so the flattened side matches the scraped section of the bore. The inside end of the plug should be flush with the edge of the notch. When the plug is in place (photograph 6), there will be a thin space between the flattened side of the plug and the scraped side of the windway (Figure A). Sighting down the plug, you should just be able to see the edge of the notch (Figure B). If the notch and plug are correctly positioned, you will hear a sound when you blow into the whistle. Further slight adjustments of the plug to increase the size of the air passage may make a dramatic difference in the whistle's tone. When you are satisfied with the tone, sand the end of the plug flush. Then bevel the end of the dowel and plug on the bottom with a rasp or pocketknife (Figure B). The whistle is now finished, but you can personalize it in some way if you like. I beveled the closed end (photograph 7) and drilled a small hole there for a neck cord. To give the whistle a smooth finish, rub it with vegetable oil.

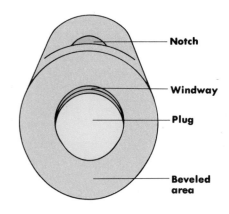

B
Figure B: An end view of the dowel whistle shows the windway with flattened plug inserted. The edge of the notch should be barely visible through the windway when viewed from this angle. Note that the bottom part of the mouth end is beveled.

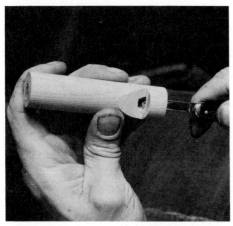

4: Use the small blade of a pocketknife to scrape the inside top of the dowel between the notch and the mouth end. This makes the hole elliptical, creating a windway when the plug is inserted.

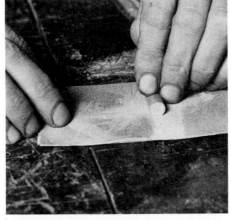

5: Slightly flatten the top side of the ⅜-inch plug by rubbing the dowel back and forth across fine sandpaper. Be careful to remove only a small amount of wood.

6: Insert the plug as far as the notch, with its flattened side matching the scraped-out top of the windway. Then try the whistle. If its tone does not please you, sand the plug a bit more.

7: If you like, you can use the file to bevel both sides of the closed end of the whistle to achieve the shape shown in Figure A.

8: To finish the dowel whistle, rub it with vegetable oil applied with a soft cloth. Let the oil soak in, then rub to remove any excess.

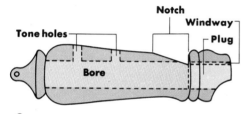

C
Figure C: A drawing of a lathe-turned hardwood whistle shows that the construction is basically the same as that of the dowel whistle. The turned whistle, however, has two finger holes and elegant contours.

9: An inch-square block of hardwood is being turned on a wood lathe to make a decoratively shaped whistle body. The result is shown in the color photograph on page 2776.

10: While the turned whistle body is still spinning on the lathe, it is easily sanded smooth.

11: After the whistle body is removed from the lathe, it is clamped in a vise while the core is drilled out with a portable power drill.

Toys and Games
A turned hardwood whistle

If you are experienced in the use of a wood lathe (as I am), you might like to try making a signal whistle of turned hardwood like the shiny black one shown on page 2776. To begin, I cut a block of African blackwood 1 inch square and 3½ inches long. As in the dowel whistle, a small piece of ⅜-inch dowel is needed for a plug, plus a ⅜-inch twist bit; a portable electric drill or drill press; a half-round file; and medium sandpaper.

Draw corner-to-corner diagonal lines on the ends of the block of blackwood to find the centers. Mount the block on the lathe at these centers, and turn it down (photograph 9) to a shape like that in Figure C. Or make one of your own design. (For wood-turning instructions, see *Creative Wood Turning* by Dale Nish, published by Brigham Young University Press). Since the turned block will be drilled with a ⅜-inch bit, maintain a minimum outside diameter of ⅝ inch for a minimum wall thickness of ⅛ inch. Sand the turned block while it is still spinning on the lathe (photograph 10).

If you use a portable electric drill, clamp the turned block in a vise and let the marked center at the mouth end be your drilling guide (photograph 11). If you use a drill press, hold the piece with a clamp while you drill. From this point, follow the steps shown in photographs 2 through 8 for making the dowel whistle: drill out the center, notch the top, and fit a plug in the windway. Once you achieve a satisfactory tone, you can drill one or two ⅛-inch holes from the top side of the whistle into the bore (Figure C). By opening or closing these with your fingers, you can play several notes. If you drill a hole too close to the notch, however, or make the holes too large (more than 3/16 inch) you may lose the tone. If this happens, you can fill the hole with wax or a glued-in wood plug and drill another hole.

As with the dowel whistle, the windway can be beveled with file and sandpaper to fit the lower lip more comfortably. I drilled a hole in the turned whistle, opposite the mouth end, for a neck cord. This whistle was rubbed with vegetable oil and buffed to a high shine.

Other Variations

A whistle can be made of almost anything. Potters make them of clay and some woodworkers whittle them into odd shapes. I have even used the bones of small animals and large birds that have been dried and bleached by the sun (page 2776).

Performing Arts
Flutes

Noted for their sweet and haunting sounds, flutes have a prominent place in rhyme and legend. The pipes of a Greek god Pan were made of reeds; Mother Goose immortalized Tom, the Piper's Son. The Pied Piper gained fame by charming all the rats out of Hamlin with his flute music, and Far Eastern fakirs have long been pretending to charm cobras out of baskets the same way. A flute can be a sophisticated orchestral instrument made of silver or a rustic bamboo shepherd's pipe (page 2780). They have been made of ivory, glass, porcelain, rubber, papier-mâché, and even wax. Shown on page 2775 are flutes I have made on a lathe from various kinds of hardwoods. But a beginning musician and amateur carpenter can make a playable, satisfying flute from inexpensive and widely available PVC tubing using only simple tools. I am playing such a flute in the picture opposite.

A Flute from PVC Tubing

To make a plastic flute, you will need a piece of PVC tubing ¾ inch in diameter and 24 inches long. Scraps this size might be available for little or nothing in hardware stores. Tools you need are: a hand or power drill; ¼- and ⅜-inch twist bits; small round file; retractable tape measure; pencil; and a cork that will fit snugly inside the tubing.

Since plastic tubing has no irregularities, finger holes can be laid out according to a formula to produce the tones for the key of D. Follow the dimensions below to mark positions for the mouth and finger holes with a tape measure and pencil. Keep all of the holes in a straight line. When you have marked the center of all the holes, fasten the pipe in a vise and use a ⅜-inch bit to drill the mouth hole. Then use a ¼-inch bit to drill the six finger holes (photograph 12). With a round file smooth any roughness or burrs from around each hole. Shape the mouth into an oval with the round file (photograph 13).

Before you will be able to sound a note, the end of the flute nearest the mouth hole must be stopped with a cork (photograph 14). The bottom edge of the cork should be ¾ inch from the center of the mouth hole. To check this measurement, insert the tape measure blade inside the flute from the open end, against the cork, and read the measurement through the mouth hole. When the cork is in the right place, the flute should sound the note D with all holes closed (use a pitch pipe or piano for tuning.)

This type of flute is called a transverse or cross-blown flute because you must blow across the mouth hole rather than into it. For some this is a difficult technique to master. But once you are able to produce a steady fundamental tone, you can tune each hole, one at a time, with the round file. If you like you can decorate the flute with any nontoxic paint that is not water soluble, such as oil or acrylic.

Books for further reading
If you wish to learn more about flutes and flute making, read **The Flute and Flute Playing** by Theobald Boehm (Dover). First published in 1871, it was written by the man who perfected the silver flute that is most widely used today. **The Amateur Wind Instrument Maker** by Trevor Robinson (University of Massachusetts Press) describes other techniques for making wind instruments.

12: Clamp the pipe in a vise and drill the mouth hole with a ⅜-inch bit, the six finger holes with a ¼-inch bit. Keep all the holes aligned.

13: Use a rattail file to shape the mouth hole into an oval, to remove any roughness in the finger holes and to tune them if necessary.

14: Fit the cork into the end of the pipe nearest the mouth hole, trimming it, if necessary, until its base is ¾ inch from the center of the mouth hole.

Flute dimensions
Total length 24 inches; inside diameter ¾ inch

From end to center of mouth hole: 3⅜ inches

From end to center of sixth finger hole: 12¼ inches

From end to center of fifth finger hole: 13⅝ inches

From end to center of fourth finger hole: 15¼ inches

From end to center of third finger hole: 17 inches

From end to center of second finger hole: 18⅜ inches

From end to center of first finger hole: 20⅛ inches

A simple flute made of plastic pipe and a cork is eminently playable, as the author demonstrates.

Ursula E. Goebel has been interested in crafts and music since her childhood in Germany, where she learned to play the recorder, a wooden end-blown flute. She was taught how to make and play bamboo shepherds' pipes by John Morgan at the Penland School of Crafts in North Carolina. She teaches the craft to children at community centers and summer camps and in adult education programs. Mrs. Goebel lives with her husband and children in Newtown, Connecticut.

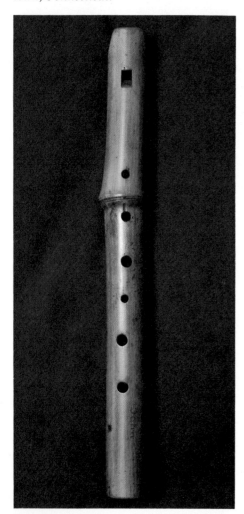

Although this bamboo shepherd's pipe looks rustic, it has been carefully tuned by hand to the key of D. This pipe is end blown, so it is easy for a beginner to produce good tones on it with a little practice.

Performing Arts
A shepherd's pipe of bamboo $ ⏱ 👫 🏃

Bamboo has been used for flute making for centuries not only because it is hollow but because it has special tonal qualities. The raw bamboo is solid at each joint, but these barriers can be bored through easily with an awl or ice pick. If you indicate that you plan to make a shepherd's pipe when you order the bamboo it will come with the center already bored in most cases.

The tools you will need are shown in photograph 15. In addition, you will need linseed oil and contact cement. The bamboo that you use must be 11½ to 12 inches long and have an inside diameter of ¾ to ⅞ inch. The walls should be about ⅛ inch thick and uncracked; bamboo is easily cracked if it is subjected to extremes of temperature or rough handling. The Bamboo and Rattan Works, 901 Jefferson St., Hoboken, New Jersey, will fill mail orders for a minimum of ten pieces. You may also be able to obtain usable bamboo at carpet, sporting goods, or garden stores. Or consult the Yellow Pages under "Bamboo." Hand selection is recommended, as it assures you of getting a perfect piece.

Ideally, a pipe would not have any of the bamboo's natural joints. If you must use a piece with joints, one of them must be at least 2 inches from one end. If the piece has a lengthwise indentation, position it on a side rather than along the top of the flute with a pencil line from end to end. Bamboo grows with coarse natural ridges so your pencil will be guided in a straight line without the use of a ruler.

Cutting the Mouthpiece
Before cutting away any part of the mouth end, press it down over the cork to leave an impression (photograph 16). Mark the impression with a pencil. Then trim the wide end of the cork to the rough inside diameter of the pipe using a penknife. Sand it smooth by rolling and turning it on sandpaper, keeping it straight and not sloping the sides in any direction. The cork should fit snugly but not tightly into the end of the pipe. You should be able to put it in and remove it easily. (If the cork is tight, it will expand with moisture and crack the bamboo.) When the cork is fitted, remove it and you are ready to make the first mouthpiece cut.

Mark the top third of the mouthpiece circle, as shown in Figure D, with a pencil. Then mark around the pipe at a point ¾ inch in from the end of the mouthpiece. On this line, mark the midpoint on both sides. Use the coping saw to cut halfway through the pipe from the underside on the line. Be careful not to cut more than halfway through. When you saw or drill, rest the bamboo in a piece of molding so it will not roll. Next, cut at an angle from the top third down to the first cut on both sides (photograph 17). This removes a section as shown in Figure E. To avoid cracking the bamboo, make a slight starting cut, then saw along the pencil line.

The Window
Mark a point centered on the top of the pipe, 1½ inches in from the mouth end. This is the center of an opening called the window (Figure F). Make an indentation at the mark with the tip of a knife to give the drill bit a starting point so it will not slip. Drill through with a 3/16-inch bit, being careful not to press so hard the bamboo splinters. Turn the drill backward to remove it. The finished window hole should be a rectangular opening 1/4 by 3/16 inch, with the wider dimension running crosswise. Square the drilled hole to these dimensions with a craft knife. Then smooth the sides of the hole by filing as shown in photograph 18.

The Air Passage
As shown in Figure G, the air passage is a squared notch cut inside the top of the mouth end, running from the window to the open end. Make guidelines for this cut by drawing pencil lines inside the pipe from the sides of the window to the outer end, following the grain of the wood. With a craft knife, gouge out a shallow groove ¼ inch wide and no deeper than 1/32 inch (photograph 19). After roughing out the groove with the knife, use a triangular file to smooth the surface. This groove is squared; it should not conform to the curve of the pipe.

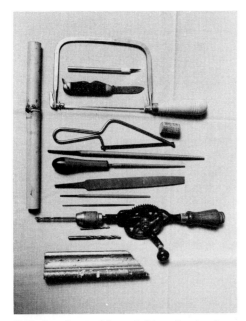

15: Tools and materials needed to make a bamboo shepherd's pipe are, from the top: coping saws, craft and pocket knives, cork, round file with ⅛-inch point, flat file 1/8 or 3/16 inch at narrow end, hand drill, 1/8- and 3/16-inch bits, a scrap of molding or a drilling block, and, at left, a segment of bamboo (opposite page).

16: Before you cut the mouthpiece, press the mouth end of the bamboo onto the cork to make an impression of the pipe's diameter. Mark the impression with a pencil. Use this mark as a guide when you trim the cork to fit snugly but not too tightly inside the mouth hole. Sand the sides of the cork evenly until the proper fit is achieved.

Repairing cracks

If your pipe cracks from rough handling or extreme temperature changes (this often happens to bamboo), lash around the cracked area with string, then cover the lashing with contact cement. Fill the crack with wood plastic or contact cement.

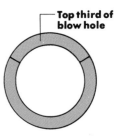

D
Figure D: Mark off one-third of the circumference of the bamboo on the mouth end, using a pencil. This will help you shape the mouthpiece.

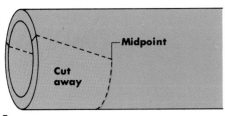

E
Figure E: Mark the segment to be cut from the mouthpiece as shown, then use a coping saw to cut along the lines.

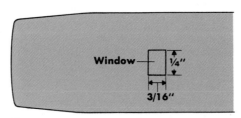

F
Figure F: To mark a rectangle for the window, first locate its center point 1½ inches from the mouth end of the pipe, then draw the tiny rectangle.

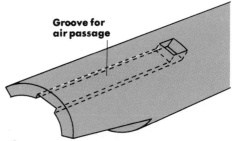

G
Figure G: Cut a square-cornered air passage into the roof of the mouth end so its width matches the width of the window. The depth should not exceed 1/32 inch at the window end.

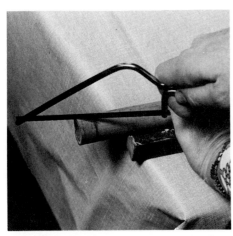

17: Using a coping saw, cut along the marked lines to shape the mouthpiece. To prevent the bamboo from rolling, rest it in a recess in the molding or drilling block while you saw.

18: After you cut the window with a drill and a craft knife, file the inner surfaces to square the corners perfectly using a steady up and down movement with a square file.

19: Cut the groove for the air passage with a craft knife, following parallel lines drawn from the sides of the window to the end of the mouthpiece. Then smooth the passage with a file.

Organizations

The Society of Woodwind Makers, P.O. Box 686, Mendocino, Calif. 95460, is a source of information on this craft and conducts instrument-building workshops.

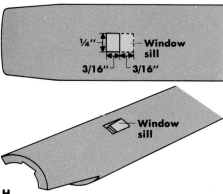

H
Figure H: Mark a window sill the same size as the window, as shown in the top drawing. Then, as shown in the lower diagram, cut the sill at a 45-degree angle to the window. Leave an inner edge 1/32 inch thick.

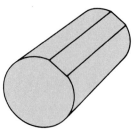

I
Figure I: Flatten one side of the cork by sanding or filing it evenly to a strip corresponding in width to the air passage cut in the pipe.

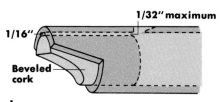

J
Figure J: Fit the cork into the mouth end of the pipe, aligning the inside end with the edge of the window. After testing to make sure you can obtain a good fundamental tone, trim the cork to fit your lower lip comfortably.

The Window Sill

On the top side, mark an area the exact dimension of the window but adjacent to it, opposite the mouth end, as shown in Figure H. This will be cut away with the craft knife at a 45-degree angle, sloping toward the window (photograph 20). The edge of this sill abutting the window should be approximately 1/32 inch thick. Do not alter the actual inside dimensions of the window as you cut the sill. If the inside edge of the sill is cut too thin, the tone will be shrill; too thick an edge will give a dull tone.

Fitting the Cork

The cork needs to be flattened along one side at a point corresponding with the air passage. First, insert the smoothest end of the cork into the pipe until it is even with the bottom of the window (Figure J). (The bottom of the window is the edge nearest the mouth end.) Twist the cork around until little or no light shows around its edges. When this is achieved, mark the position of the air passage on the cork (photograph 21). Remove the cork and file it flat along the side that you have marked, to correspond with the air passage groove (Figure J). Do not make a hollow or let the side slope down toward the inside of the pipe. When the cork is reinserted, there should not be more than a 1/32-inch opening at the window end of the air passage and at least 1/16 inch at the mouth end (Figure J).

With the cork flush with the top edge of the window, slice off the excess cork so it is also flush with the mouth end. The underside of the cork can then be cut away at an angle until it is comfortable in your mouth (Figure J). But do not cut it flush with the bamboo as you may wish to remove it to make a slight adjustment in the air passage during tuning. When you blow into the pipe with the cork in place, you should produce a good fundamental tone. If it sounds too thin, slightly enlarge the air passage, but not to more than 1/16 inch. This pipe will be tuned to the key of D, so the first note sounded should be C#. If it is C, the pipe is too long. Cut a 1/4-inch

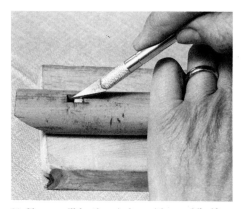

20: Shape a sill for the window with a craft knife, cutting a notch that tapers toward the window at 45-degree angle.

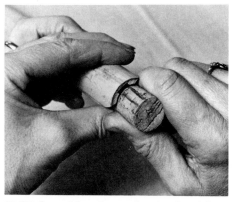

21: Fit the cork into the mouth end and mark lines matching the air passage with a pencil. Use sandpaper or a file to flatten the cork.

22: Hold the pipe in playing position to determine placement of the tuning hole, which will be cut under the little finger of the right (lower) hand.

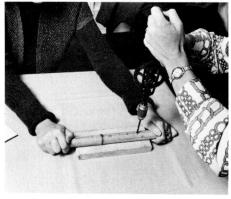

23: When you drill the finger holes, rest the pipe in a groove in the molding and have a helper hold it steady as you drill.

ring off the bottom end of the pipe and check again against a piano or pitch pipe. You may need to cut off some amount between ¼ and 1 inch to achieve a C#. Proceed carefully, slicing one thin ring at a time until C# is achieved. (It will be D when a tuning hole is cut.)

Marking and Drilling Holes

All but two of the eight holes will be drilled along the pencil line you have drawn down the top of the pipe. Mark the bottom hole (called the first) at a point one-fourth of the total distance from the bottom of the pipe to the middle of the window (Figure K). The sixth hole, closest to the window, should be at least 2½ inches from the middle of the window. Any ring in the bamboo has to be taken into account here; even if you must be inexact, it is better not to drill into a ring. Mark these two holes with a pencil along the center line and cut an indentation for the drill bit at each point with a knife. Mark the remaining holes, spacing them as you wish between the first and sixth holes but making the distance between the first and second slightly greater than between the others. When all the holes have been marked and notched along the center line, hold the pipe with your fingers placed on the marks for the holes, left hand nearest the mouth end (photograph 22). The thumb of the left hand supports the pipe from underneath, directly opposite the index finger that plays the sixth (top) hole. The index, middle, and fourth fingers of the right hand play the third, second, and first holes respectively. As you hold the pipe in this position, note where the little finger of the right hand falls naturally and mark this spot. Also note where the left thumb falls and mark that spot. The seventh and eighth holes will be drilled at these points.

The Tuning Hole

The hole to be drilled where the little finger falls is the tuning hole; make it first, using a ⅛-inch bit. Notch it, then drill very carefully so the drill does not pierce the other side (photograph 23). When this hole is open and the pipe sounded, the note you hear should be D. If the pitch needs to be raised, use a small round file to enlarge the hole, working slowly and carefully until the D sounds.

The First through Sixth Holes

Drill the first hole next, using a 3/16-inch bit. All the holes will need some adjustment with the round file to achieve the proper pitch so a scale can be played. Tune each just after it is drilled. Drill the second hole with the 3/16-inch bit and enlarge it as necessary. This is likely to be the largest hole but don't judge by looks, only by sound. When it gives you an F#, practice a bit on the first two holes. It is a good idea to accustom yourself to the sounds of the notes gradually as you drill the holes. Drill the third hole with a ⅛-inch bit. This is smaller because it is a half note. Again, bring it up to the right pitch with the round file. Drill the rest of the top holes (4, 5, and 6) with a 3/16-inch bit and file each to the right pitch, one at a time. For the seventh hole on the back of the pipe, use a ⅛-inch bit; this too is a small half-note hole. If a hole happens to get too big, making its pitch too high, you can partially fill the hole with contact cement. When the glue gets tacky, pierce it with a pencil and push the glue to the rim to line the hole, thus making it smaller.

Tuning Tips

When you blow into the pipe, say "Te" to position your tongue correctly. When tuning a finger hole, hold the pipe at a relaxed 45-degree angle. If you raise the pipe while blowing, the pitch will change; holding it steady keeps the pitch constant. Practice blowing with a steady pressure because you can only tune correctly if your breath pressure is constant. Starting at the bottom, tune one hole at a time as it is drilled. Enlarging it slightly with a file will raise the pitch; if a hole gets too large it can be made smaller by lining it with contact cement.

Finishing Touches

Glue the cork in place, being careful not to clog the air passage. Rub the pipe with linseed oil frequently to keep it from drying out. Oil the inside with an oily cotton rag wrapped around a file. Also oil the rims of the holes.

For related entries, see "Dulcimers," "Music Making," "Stagecraft," and "Wind Harps."

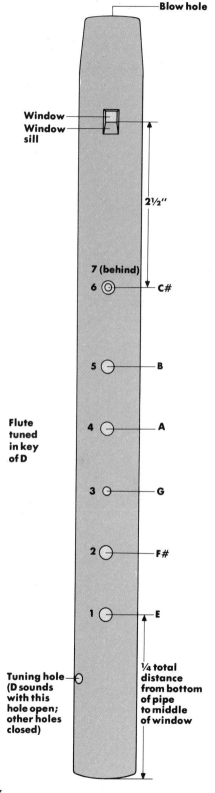

K

Figure K: This diagram of the complete bamboo pipe shows the approximate placement and size of finger holes. However, because of the irregularities in bamboo, each pipe you make will be slightly different, and each finger hole must be individually tuned by filing.

Eolian Harp.

Mr URBAN,

HAving lately been very much entertain'd with an instrument commonly known by the name of *Eolus's Harp*, and imagining it not to be thoroughly known, I could not but think it would be agreeable to many of your readers to have a description of it, especially as the contrivance is so simple, that the chief part of it may be easily made by a common carpenter.

Procure a box to be made of as thin deal as possible, (*Fig.* I.) the length exactly the width of the sash, where you intend to fix it, the depth of the box 5 or 6 inches, and the width 7 or 8 inches; let there be glued upon it at *a a*, two pieces of wainscot about half an inch high, and a quarter of an inch thick, and within side let there be glued to the top at each end, under *b b*, two pieces of beach, about an inch square, and the length the width of the box; then let there be made through the top, and into these pieces, as many small holes as you would have strings to the instrument, half at one end and half at the other, into which fix the same number of pins, such as are us'd in harpsicords, &c. all that remains now is to string it with small catgut strings, or blue first fiddle strings, fixing one end to a small brass pin as at *e e*, (*Fig.* II.) and twisting the other round the opposite pin as at *b b*.

When these strings are tun'd at unisons, and the instrument plac'd with the strings outward, in the window to which it is fitted, provided the wind blows upon the window, it will give a sound like a distant choir, increasing or decreasing according to the strength of the wind.

c c in *Fig.* I. are only sound holes cut in the top of the box, and the thinner the top is, the better will the instrument perform. *I am, Sir, Yours &c.*

A. Z.

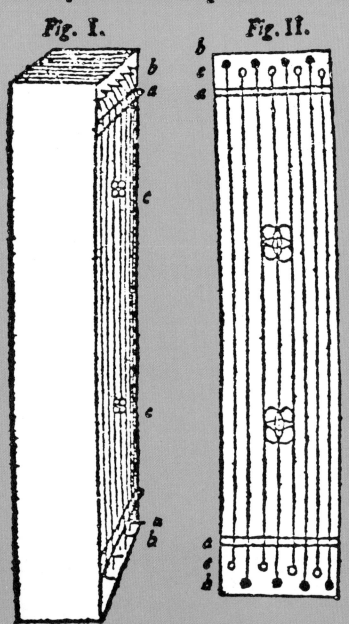

Fig. I.   *Fig.* II.

WIND HARPS

There's Music in the Air

From the whispering of a summer breeze to a blizzard's howling crescendo, the eloquence of the wind has long fascinated all who lend an ear. It is not surprising that the wind was endowed with a personality in many mythologies—and that ancient words for wind are often the same as those for breath, spirit, mind, life, or to-play-a-musical-instrument. In fact, some aficionados of the wind's music developed a remarkable instrument that is played entirely by the wind. Perfected since 1550 but modeled on an ancient progenitor, it is called the wind harp or Aeolian harp, in honor of Aeolus, Greek god of the winds.

The haunting melody of the wind harp created quite a stir in its day. Its popularity started during the late Renaissance and did not die until around 1900. Only a handful of antique harps are still in existence, most of them mute in museum cases. But the original makers left clear instructions (for example, the facsimile, opposite), so if you like you can make a simple but authentic instrument, place it on a windowsill, and fill your home with its enchanting tones—even if you know nothing about music.

A Diverse Background

Wind harps have existed in various forms in Ethiopia, Java, South Africa, among the Indians of Guyana, and at the imperial court of ancient China. According to one legend, the principle of the Aeolian harp was discovered when the Greek god Hermes heard the wind playing on some animal sinews he had stretched across a tortoise shell to dry. Another story attributes the discovery to King David who, being in the habit of hanging his lyre above his bed when he slept, awoke one night to sublime strains plucked on his lyre by the wind. In Indonesia it is believed that music fills the world and that musicians and instruments simply make audible what is going on all the time. In the same vein, Shakespeare and many others referred to "music of the spheres" and, of course, science recognizes many sounds beyond human hearing range. To those who have heard the wind harp, the existence of hidden music is not at all fantastic.

Admirers

There have been many references to wind harps in world literature. They were hailed in poetic terms by Spenser, Smollet, Coleridge, Keats, Tennyson, Emerson, Thoreau, Melville, and Verne. Their special quality is conveyed in descriptions like these: "The Aeolian harp produces enchanting tones which defy description, like the sound of distant choirs, rising gently and dying away again, more like a melodious vision of heavenly Nature than the result of human artifice;" "Entirely free from all interference of art, it thus leads to a higher magic, under whose influence sensitive men yield to innocent pleasure, however much their wakeful reason may protest;" "It is not simply an aural perception of beauty—it is the very heart which listens to the music." If you wish to hear a wind harp before making one, a recording is available from Sound Image, Amherst, Massachusetts. For additional reading, there is an interesting anthology, *Aeolian Harp*, edited by Stephen Bonner and published in England in 1970.

Building Requirements

Records from the past describe six types of European wind harps. Some are complicated, but a few are quite simple to make. The two projects that follow are based on a single model; they differ only in that the first (page 2786) uses a sound board and few strings, while the second (page 2791) has a sound box and more strings. The simpler model is a good beginning project but it requires a brisk wind and

Paul Dixon, a professional harpsichord maker and woodworker, spends his spare time making wind harps and restoring old violins at his home in Wayland, Massachusetts. Wood and stringed instruments have interested him from his early youth.

Opposite: This letter to the editor of *Gentleman's Magazine*, London, was published in February, 1754. In it, an anonymous reader gives admirably clear instructions and diagrams for making a wind harp, which he called Eolus's Harp. The Aeolian harp, played by the wind alone, was virtually forgotten by 1900 but is being revived.

produces only a limited range of tones. The second model is a sophisticated instrument in the classical tradition which produces a gamut of rich tones in a gentle breeze.

An Aeolian harp needs to be solidly built but light for portability and resonance. Figure A shows the basic structure and names the parts. Some sound boxes have no sound hole; others have as many as three. The number of strings can range from four to 20. Pine, maple, or mahogany can be used for the sound box; in addition to these, beech or spruce can be used for the box ends and window stops. The bridges must be of oak or similarly hard wood. The strings and their hitch pins and tuning pins are the kind used in harpsichords, but an instrument less than 30 inches long needs nylon strings.

How Music is Produced

To picture how the harp works, imagine water in a stream flowing past a protruding rock. The water is broken into many whirlpools and eddies. The same thing happens when a current of air passes a string on a wind harp. A train of small whirlwinds is produced, and these strike the string repeatedly, causing it to vibrate and sound a musical note. Some wind harps have several strings tuned to a number of different notes by varying their length. But most modern wind harps are like a guitar with strings of the same length but of varying thicknesses and tension. (This method is used in the projects that follow.) The wind harp's extraordinary sound has to do with the number of tones that make up its chord. The first ten are familiar harmonics. But if the wind is strong enough, it will excite an eleventh, a twelfth, and higher vibrations, and these produce the weird, unearthly Aeolian tones. For tips on tuning wind harps, see pages 2790 and 2793.

A

Figure A: Wind harps come in a number of different forms, but the basic parts that are common to most of them are shown in this drawing. A window stop at each end protects the instrument and holds the window sash at the proper height. In an otherwise hollow box, thick end blocks provide a firm foundation for the tuning and hitch pins, which hold the strings taut over movable triangular bridges. A hole in the sound box increases the resonance.

A simplified wind harp can be constructed on a solid base board rather than a hollow sound box, and can be made with as few as five strings. When the instrument is sandwiched between a window sash and sill, its strings vibrate and produce harmonious sounds in a strong breeze.

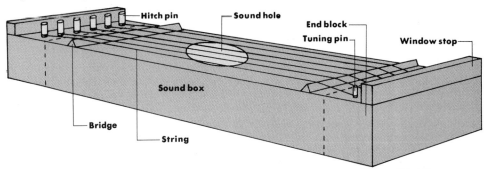

Environmental Projects
A simplified wind harp

To make the simple wind harp pictured at the bottom of the opposite page, you will need a base board of wood such as cherry, maple, or birch 1¼ inches thick, 3 inches wide, and 1 inch shorter than the width of the window where it will be used. The model shown is 31 inches long. Also needed are: two window stops of wood, ½ by ¾ by 3 inches (I used walnut); two triangular bridges of hard wood such as ebony, oak, or rosewood, 3 inches long and ½ inch high; five hitch pins; five tuning pins; a tuning hammer; five nylon, steel, or brass strings (page 2789); a crosscut saw and ripsaw for cutting across and with wood grain; clamps; pencil; ruler or square; protractor; hand or power drill with No. 10 and No. 58 bits; small hand plane (optional); wood chisel; triangular file; hammer; fine sandpaper; and all-purpose white glue.

The Base Board

Any unwarped wood that is fairly hard can be used for the base. Its overall dimensions are not critical if it fits easily in the window and is wide enough for the tuning and hitch pins, as indicated in Figure B. To determine the ideal length, measure the width of the window opening and subtract 1 inch. If you make the harp much shorter, too much of the wind's force will be diverted from the strings. As for pin spacing, the arrangement shown is not the only one possible, but it is one that works. The base should be at least 1¼ inches thick so the pins that hold the strings can be set 1 inch deep.

Once you have a smooth base board, use a pencil and ruler or square to draw lines across the board 1¼ inches from each end and a third line 1¾ inches from one end (Figure B). On the end with a single line, mark five points on the line at ½-inch intervals, the middle point centered on the board (photograph 1 and Figure B). (If your board is 3 inches wide, the end points will fall ½ inch from an edge.) At the other end, mark these points on the outer line at 1-inch intervals, centering the middle point, and two points on the inner line an inch apart, each ½ inch from the center (photograph 2 and Figure B).

Drilling Holes

Clamp the base board securely to your workbench, using a wood scrap to keep the clamp jaw from marring the wood. Using a hand or power drill and a No. 58 bit (.042-inch diameter), prepare to drill holes 1 inch deep for the hitch pins at each of the five marked points. Put masking tape around the drill bit 1 inch from the tip to help you gauge when you have drilled deeply enough. Drill these holes at right angles to the board's surface. Then change to a No. 10 bit (.193-inch diameter) to drill the tuning-pin holes, and tape as before. Because the strings will be twisted around the tuning pins (not looped), they will meet the edges of the pins rather than the centers. So these holes will need to be positioned differently to make the strings

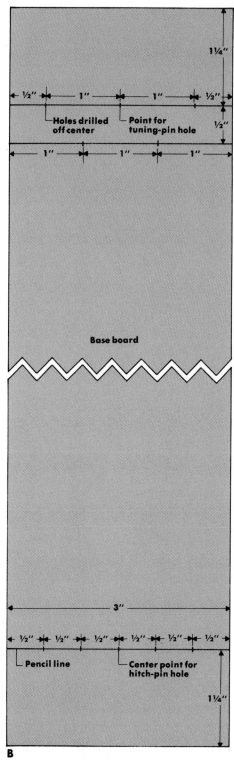

B

Figure B: In the simplified wind harp with a board for a base, mark the holes for the tuning and hitch pins as indicated. Draw lines across the base board 1¼ inches from one end and 1¼ and 1¾ inches from the other end. Mark the single line every ½ inch and the double lines alternately at the same interval. The holes for the straight row of hitch pins will be drilled on the marks, but those for the staggered tuning pins will be drilled at one side of the marks, since the strings will be wrapped around those pins.

1: Determine the centers for hitch-pin holes by drawing a line across the sound board 1¼ inches in from the end and marking the line five times at ½-inch intervals, with the middle point at the center of the board and the end points equidistant from the edges.

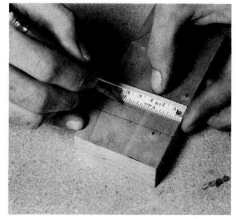

2: To locate tuning-pin holes, draw two lines across the base board 1¼ and 1¾ inches from the other end. Mark the lines alternately at ½-inch intervals with five points (three on the outer line, two on the inner) so the five correspond to those for the hitch pins.

3: Drill holes 1 inch deep for the tuning pins using a No. 10 bit. Tilt the drill as shown—about 10 degrees—toward the end of the board. Drill all these holes at one side of the pencil marks so the strings will be parallel with the board's edge.

parallel the sides of the board. Place the instrument in front of you with the tuning-pin end on your left. Drill the tuning-pin holes so their near edges—not their centers—touch the points marked. In addition, try to hold the drill at a 10-degree angle, tilted slightly toward the end of the board. You can check this angle, visible in photograph 3, with a protractor.

Window Stops

Before inserting the tuning and hitch pins, attach the window stops to the base board. These blocks of wood (Figure A, page 2786) protect the instrument from being damaged by the window and control the position of the sash relative to the strings. Cut two pieces of ½-by-¾-inch wood to equal the width of the base board. Sand the pieces smooth without rounding their corners. Attach them (with a ½-inch edge down) to the ends of the base board using white glue and clamps (photograph 4). Before the glue dries, wipe off any excess. After an hour, remove the clamps and use a chisel to scrape away any hardened glue from the inside corners. With a small plane, chamfer the inside edge of each stop (photograph 5); this is optional and purely decorative. Sand the instrument smooth with fine sandpaper and apply a finish. Wax or varnish are attractive finishes and provide a measure of waterproofing. If you prefer, brush on boiled linseed oil, wiping off any excess that remains on the surface after 20 minutes.

Tuning Pins and Hitch Pins

When the finish is dry, insert the tuning pins (Figure C) into the five larger holes. They should fit so tightly you can advance them into their holes only by rotating them on their threads. Use a harpsichord or auto-harp tuning hammer (photograph 6) to turn each pin until it is nearly tight, just beyond the point where the threaded part disappears into the hole. (The tuning hammer is a kind of wrench that fits over the square head of the tuning pin.) At this point, the top of the pin should be just below the top of the window blocks.

Insert five hitch pins into the remaining holes. These should also fit tightly and will have to be hammered into the holes. Hold a scrap of wood ⅜ inch thick next to the started pins, and drive them in until the tops of the pins are even with the surface of the wood (photograph 7).

4: Using white glue, attach a window stop at each end of the base board, narrow edge down. Clamp the stops, as shown, for an hour.

5: Remove the clamps, and use a small hand plane to chamfer the inner edge of the window blocks to a depth of about ⅛ inch. (This is optional.)

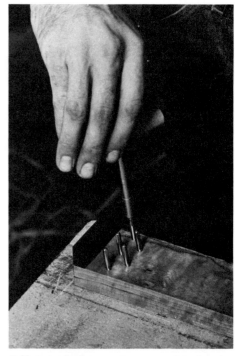

6: Use a tuning hammer to screw each tuning pin into the base board until the threaded part of the shank is no longer visible.

The Strings

The strings may be of steel, brass, or nylon as long as they are the unwound type; twined strings do not work well on wind harps. Ask for two each of the first two strings for a guitar (or larger instrument), and one of the third string—that is, two Es, two Bs, and a G. An alternative that works well is low-stretch nylon fishing line. To produce three distinct notes, use 30-, 40-, and 60-pound test line. With either system, string the five tuning pins in this sequence: on the first and fourth pins (starting from either side), put the lightest string; on the second and fifth, the medium-weight string; and on the third, the heaviest string.

Attach the strings first to the hitch pins, then to the tuning pins. To knot the end that slips over the hitch pin, double it back on itself to form a small loop (photograph 8). Then twist the doubled line four or five times (photograph 9). Insert the string end back through the loop (photograph 10). Drop the loop over the hitch pin and pull the end of the string taut. Then take the free end of the string to the other end of the base board and through the hole in the corresponding tuning pin. Wind the string loosely once around the pin in a clockwise direction. Insert the free end between the pin and the loop thus produced. Pull the string end taut, tighten the tuning pin until the string has lost its slack, and cut off the excess string.

The Bridges

The two bridges (of the hardest wood obtainable) should run the full width of the base board, with a triangular cross section ½ inch from base to apex. To produce such a shape, cut a piece of 1-by-1-inch lumber diagonally; then plane and sand until the height of each bridge is ½ inch.

Slip the bridges under the strings about 4 inches from each end of the base board. At this distance, the bridge on the tuning-pin end should make the strings extend out at right angles from the backward-slanting pins. Adjust the bridge as necessary to establish this relationship. With a pencil, mark where the strings pass over the bridges (photograph 11). Then remove the bridges and use the corner of a triangular file to make small grooves at these points (photograph 12). Lubricate each groove with graphite from a soft lead pencil. When the bridges are put in place, with the strings in the grooves, the tension of the strings will hold the bridges in place.

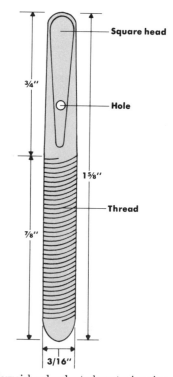

C

Figure C: Harpsichord and auto-harp tuning pins, made of metal, are about 1 5/8 inches long and 3/16 inch in diameter. The top of the pin is square to fit a tuning hammer—like a bolt head in a wrench. There is a small hole near the top for a string to be inserted. The lower part of the pin is threaded so it can be turned into its hole to adjust the tension of the string.

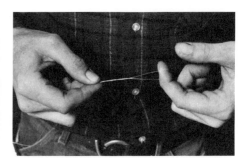

7: With a hammer, drive the hitch pins into their holes. Place a block of wood ⅜ inch thick beside the pins so they all will project that far.

8: To tie a string to a hitch pin, first loop one end of the string over a finger, and hold the doubled line in the other hand.

9: Next, rotate the finger holding the loop four or five times to form a twist in the doubled string in either direction.

10: Finally, slip the short loose end back through the finger loop, drop the loop over the hitch pin, and pull the knot tight.

11: When the triangular bridges are in place, mark the points on their top edges where the strings pass over them.

12: Remove the bridges and file small grooves at the points marked. Lubricate these grooves with graphite from a soft pencil.

Use and Care of the Harp

There are a number of approaches to tuning. The simplest is to tune all the strings to the same pitch. Select a note arbitrarily. Any note will do if the strings are loose enough to vibrate when plucked and taut enough to continue vibrating for a time. Tune the strings by twisting the tuning pins in turn until the same note sounds on each string when it is lightly plucked. Alternatively, tune some of the strings to the same note an octave higher. If you are familiar with music, you may want to experiment by tuning the strings to other intervals—fourths, fifths, or diatonically.

Place the harp on a windowsill on a windy day, and lower the sash gently onto the window blocks. To obtain the maximum breeze, open a door or window on an opposite wall. The greater the movement of air, the more sound will be produced. You may have to wait patiently until the wind is right. But if no sound is produced by a strong gust, adjust the tension of the strings or the position of the bridges until a distinct sound can be heard.

Protect your instrument from moisture damage. Since you will want to try it during stormy weather, wipe away any raindrops with a clean, soft cloth when you finish using the harp. Do not leave it permanently in the window. A screw eye in one end will let you hang the harp on a wall when it is not in use.

Near right: This nineteenth-century instrument from England is one of two Aeolian harps in the Crosby Brown musical instrument collection of New York's Metropolitan Museum of Art. It had 12 strings (11 at present) on two rows of tuning pins, two sound holes, and pentagonal bridges.

Far right: The second Aeolian harp in the Metropolitan Museum collection is also from nineteenth-century England. It is unusual in having no sound hole at all and is decorated with hand-carved bridges. It once had nine strings on a single row of tuning pins set into a raised end block.

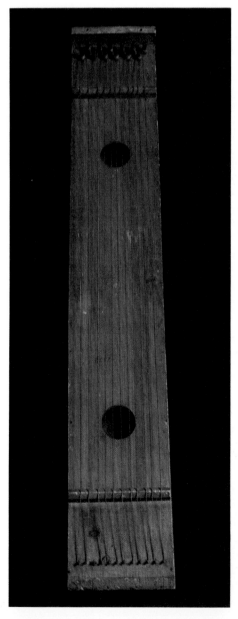
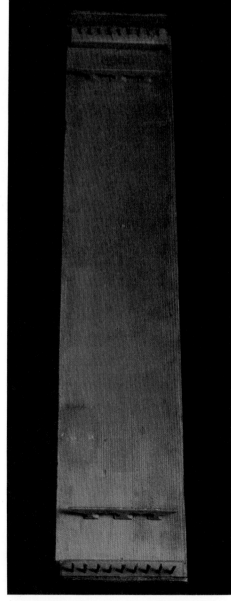

Environmental Projects
A true Aeolian harp

The progression from a simple wind harp with a single board supporting strings to a traditional Aeolian harp consists of substituting a sound box for the base board and increasing the number of strings. Most of the techniques are the same, except construction of the box is more work. The tools and materials are as listed on page 2787, but 12 tuning pins, hitch pins, and strings are used instead of five, and the box requires the specially cut wood prepared for use in musical instruments. An 8-penny finishing nail and a craft knife are also needed.

The Sound Box
To produce the proper acoustical effect, the wood used for the sound box must be straight grained and cut so the growth rings are perpendicular to its face. This kind of wood, known as quartersawn, is rarely available from lumber dealers, but can often be purchased at guitar and harpsichord shops. Ask for ¼-inch spruce, pine, or mahogany in a length equal to 1 inch less than the width of your window opening.

A wind harp with a hollow sound box will produce ethereal tones that vary with the intensity of the wind. Although some wind harps work out-doors—one outstanding example was installed on a mountaintop in Vermont—this model plays best at home, in concentrated drafts on a windowsill (page 2793).

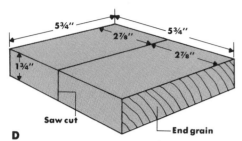

D

Figure D: Cut the end blocks from a single piece of wood 5¾ by 5¾ by 1¾ inches. Saw across the grain at the middle, as shown, so both blocks have the end grain exposed on their long edge. A third block, 2 or 3 inches long, and 1¾ inches high, taken perhaps from the original piece of wood, will be helpful later as a planing guide.

Buy enough to cut two pieces 6¼ inches wide for the top and bottom and two pieces 2 inches wide for the sides. (The actual thickness of nominal ¼-inch wood is less than 3/16 inch.) Cut the ends of the box, in the form of blocks, from harder wood such as beech, maple, or cherry. A piece 5¾ inches square and 1¾ inches thick will provide enough wood for both ends, but buy 2 or 3 inches of extra length so you will have a scrap left over. Saw this board down to a 5¾-inch square, and plane all six faces smooth. Then cut the square in half, sawing across the grain so the end grain is exposed (Figure D).

Next cut the two box sides to the length determined by the width of your window. Place the pieces side by side, and use an adjustable square to mark the ends before cutting (photograph 13). Use all-purpose white glue and clamps to attach the sides to the smallest faces of the end blocks (photograph 14). Blocks and sides should be flush on the bottom, but if other edges of the side pieces overlap the blocks slightly, they can be planed down later to a perfect fit. When the glue has dried (about an hour), remove the clamps and plane the top edges of the sides down to the blocks. Use the leftover scrap of the block as a planing guide (photograph 15). Next, attach the top and bottom pieces of the box to the ends and sides, using white glue and clamps as before. Be sure to glue the top edges of the sides to the top and bottom pieces. In assembling, let the slight excess extend evenly on all four sides—to be planed off later.

When the glue is dry, plane the side edges of the top and bottom until they are even with the box sides. A planing guide is not needed. Clamp the ends of the box, one after the other, to the workbench, and plane the ends of the box tops and sides (photograph 16). Use an extremely sharp block plane, and work in from the corners.

13: To cut sides of a sound box square and a uniform length, place them side by side when you mark the length. Draw lines across the ends of both pieces at once. Cut with a craft knife.

14: Glue the box sides to the end blocks, allowing a slight overlap on ends and tops that you will plane away later for a perfect fit. Clamp both ends, as shown, for an hour.

15: With a sharp block plane, remove the slight bit of excess wood along the edges of the box sides, using as a guide a scrap of wood the same thickness as the end blocks.

16: Clamp the box ends to the workbench, as shown, and use a sharp block plane to remove the slight overlap at both ends of the box. Plane from the corners to forestall fraying.

17: To cut the sound hole, drive a nail and a craft-knife blade through a scrap of soft wood, 1⅜ inches apart. Insert the nail point into a hole in the exact center of the sound-box top.

18: Rotate the scrap around the nail with light pressure until the disk is cut completely through by the blade. Then remove the disk by pulling it up with a nail fitted into the center hole.

The Tuning Pins and Hitch Pins

Tuning pins and hitch pins will be inserted into the ends of the instrument as they were in the previous project (page 2788). The only difference is the number—12 of each are used instead of five—and the relative placement of the pins. For the hitch-pin holes, draw a line across the top of the sound box 1¼ inches in from one end (Figure E). On the line, mark points for drilling 12 evenly spaced holes, 7/16 inch apart, in the symmetrical arrangement shown in Figure E. For the tuning-pin holes, draw three lines across the opposite end of the sound box, 1, 1½, and 2 inches in from the edge (Figure E). On these lines, mark points for 12 corresponding holes, but locate the first, fourth, seventh, and tenth on the outer line; the second, fifth, eighth, and eleventh on the middle line; and the remaining four on the inner line (Figure E).

Drill the holes as described on page 2787. Following the instructions on page 2788, attach window blocks to the ends of the sound box. Then cut a sound hole in the top of the box. Locate the center of the box and make a small hole there with an 8-penny finishing nail or a drill bit of equivalent diameter. Drive the nail through the center of a scrap of soft wood about 1 by 1 by 3 inches so its point projects. Then gently hammer a craft-knife blade through the scrap 1⅝ inches from the nail until the blade point protrudes about ¼ inch. Insert the nail in the hole in the center of the sound box, and use it as a pivot point as you rotate the wood scrap (photograph 17). The knife blade will slowly cut a circular groove in the top of the sound box. After several rotations, a disk-shaped cutout will be produced. Remove the circular scrap by lifting it with a nail in the center hole (photograph 18). After you apply a water-resistant finish, insert the tuning and hitch pins in their holes (page 2788).

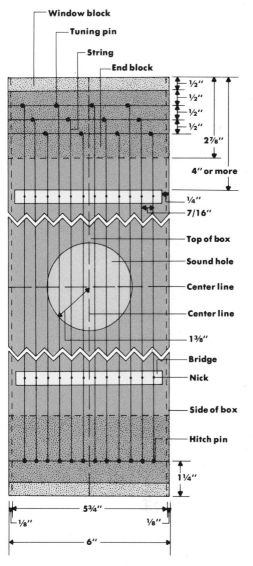

The Aeolian harp described here captures a breeze on a windowsill. The window sash is lowered onto protective blocks at the ends of the sound box. In a good crosswind, the room is filled with sound; each new breeze produces a different combination of tones.

Stringing the Harp

String the Aeolian harp as described on page 2789, except that here, use four strings of each of the recommended thicknesses—whether guitar strings or fishing line. Fit each group of four adjacent pins with string of the same weight.

Beneath the strings, insert bridges ½ inch shorter than the width of the sound box and groove them with a file (page 2789). The bridges must be at least 4 inches from each end, but their best positions will vary with the sound box and can be determined by experimenting. The tuning, use, and care of the harp are described on page 2790. If you make a wind harp that has a sound box, you can find its natural frequency by holding the instrument up and singing to it. You will find a certain note—usually a low G—to which the instrument responds by vibrating. The best results can be obtained by tuning all the strings to this note.

For related projects and crafts, see "Dulcimers," "Music Making," "Weather Forecasting," and "Whistles and Flutes."

E

Figure E: For best results, the dimensions and placement of the Aeolian harp's parts should be exactly as shown here. The window blocks, in red, and the end blocks (to the left of the points) should be set flush with the box ends. The tuning pins and corresponding hitch pins are evenly spaced 7/16 inch apart, so the strings will all be parallel and equidistant. (The staggered holes for the tuning pins, however, should be displaced as shown in Figure B.) Center the movable triangular bridges (blue) between the box sides, and place them at least 4 inches from the box ends; then make nicks on their top edges where the strings cross them. Cut the sound hole in the exact center of the box.

WINE MAKING
In Good Spirits

The juice of your favorite fruit—or flower, grain, herb, or vegetable—can be used to make wine with a pleasing taste, distinctive bouquet, and rich color. When yeast is mixed with fruit juice or other liquid containing sugar, a chemical change, fermentation, occurs. As the yeast ferments, it converts sugar to ethyl alcohol and carbon dioxide. Once all of the sugar has been converted, or the yeast reaches its alcohol tolerance level, fermentation is complete and the wine is ready for bottling. It is best to age most home wines at least a year before uncorking them for serving.

Good wine has an appealing taste that has been celebrated through the ages. Wine, good and bad, also has a history of medicinal and disinfectant uses. Sometimes it was substituted for water when the water supply was polluted. Ancient peoples discovered that some foods could be preserved by soaking them in a wine marinade. Wine was used to cleanse wounds. Its often mystifying properties led it to have an important role in many religious rituals.

In the eighteenth century, improvements in keeping wine palatable made it valued the world over as a beverage. The biggest improvement was made by a blind monk, Dom Pérignon, who promoted the use of corks for sealing bottles. (At that time, corks were being used only on the Iberian peninsula, where cork trees grew.) In a corked bottle, laid on its side, the wine could breathe as it gradually aged to perfection. A mechanical invention, the bottle screw, made it possible to put a cork in a bottle with a seal tight enough to prevent spoilage and evaporation. In the middle of the century, a sturdier, thick-walled bottle was developed.

A trio of wine makers enjoys the fruits of their labors. Richard Walters, left, a veteran wine maker, proposes a toast. His shop offers supplies and advice for the home wine maker. He and his son, Tom (right), expanded their main store in Allentown, Pennsylvania, into a nationwide franchise called Wine Hobby, U.S.A. Nily Rudner (center) started making wine when she managed the Allentown store. After doing demonstrations, she taught a course in wine making at Northampton County Community College, in Pennsylvania.

This tapestry dating from the beginning of the sixteenth century pictures French villagers gathering grapes. The grapes are placed in large wooden tubs; then they are crushed to make wine.

Opposite: Grapes, raspberries, even dried rose petals can be used to make wine at home. Nowadays most wine is bottled in glass, but for centuries, wooden casks like the one at right were used to store and transport wine. The wine would be drawn from the cask into a glass carafe for serving. The tulip-shaped wine glass, shown filled with homemade wine, is the best type for serving wine at the table.

This is a graphic interpretation of *The Expert Taster*, a painting by the nineteenth-century Belgian artist Jan David Col. Here, a wine taster is shown sampling a glass of wine in a wine cellar. To taste a glass of wine hold it up to the light to observe its brilliant colors. Then aerate the wine by rotating it gently in the glass. This acts to release any acid taste and to heighten the wine's bouquet.

Home wine making became a popular pastime as a result of these advances and the availability of sterilizing agents. Since most commercial wines are made from grapes, you may never have tasted the folk wines that you can make from other fruits, flowers, herbs, vegetables, or grains. Until recently, making wine at home was mainly a way to stretch a budget. Fresh fruits in season, inexpensive at a market or gathered in a garden, would go into jams, jellies, and wines.

On the following pages are the basic techniques for making wine from seasonal grapes. Using a similar process, you can make wine at any time of the year from canned fruit concentrates, frozen foods, or dried plant leaves, using the folk wine recipes on pages 2804 and 2805. Making wine at home requires little money, equipment, or labor. But it does require a permit (which is free), absolute cleanliness, a cool storage place, and patience. It also requires some care to avoid injury in case a bottle does burst—do not seal bottles until fermentation has ended, and store them where flying fragments of glass will be contained in the event of an explosion.

Legalities

In the United States, before you make wine for family use you must register with the federal Bureau of Alcohol, Tobacco and Firearms, filling out two copies of Form No. 1541. There are regional offices of the bureau in San Francisco, Dallas, Atlanta, Chicago, Cincinnati, Philadelphia, and New York. Or call a federal information center to get the address of the nearest field office; these offices are located in most major cities. To get a permit, you must be head of a household, and the wine you make can be used only for home consumption, not sold. After the forms are approved, one copy will be returned to you. Keep a record of the quantity of wine you make and the date. The law allows the home wine maker to make up to 200 gallons of wine each year.

Wine-Making Materials

As you gain experience in wine making, you will want to scout markets for ingredients suitable for making seasonal folk wines.

But even if it's the middle of December when you want to make a strawberry wine, don't despair. Fruits and berries available frozen can be used. Simply let the fruit thaw completely before proceeding. Also, grape and other fruit concentrates are available at wine hobby stores for wine making. With canned concentrates, a table wine can be made with ease. Many of the concentrates incorporate some of the essential ingredients and already have the right acid balance; so study the label. You may need to add only water, yeast, yeast nutrient, and sugar to start the fermentation. Packages of dried flowers, berries, and herbs sold at health food stores and wine hobby shops are also suitable for wine making. To use dried materials, steep them in boiling water for a few hours until the fragrance is strong; then let the mixture cool before you proceed with making the wine.

You may have many of the materials on hand that you will need to make wine. Wine hobby shops stock most of the necessary equipment and ingredients (photograph 1). When you gather supplies, avoid containers and equipment made of iron, brass, or copper, or any crockery glazed with lead, as these can be affected by acids in the brew. Plastic containers are ideal, but unless they are white the coloring dye may mix with the wine. You can find some of the supplies you need at a drugstore or supermarket.

To sterilize equipment you will need: sodium metabisulphate in powdered form; an empty, gallon-sized jar with a lid; rags or paper towels; and a funnel. For extracting juice you will need: two empty three-gallon-sized containers, such as white polyethylene plastic buckets; a wooden masher; a wooden spoon; a muslin or nylon bag large enough to hold several pounds of raw material; and a strainer. When you make wine in small batches, your hands will suffice to crush and press the raw material. But to make wine in quantities of five gallons or more, use a manual crusher and presser, such as the one shown in photograph 2, or an electric juice extractor. As your interest in home wine making increases, you can acquire this equipment in stages. To measure the juice for sugar and alcohol content, use a hydrometer graduated with alcohol, sugar, and specific gravity scales, and a clear vial large enough to hold the hydrometer. A kit for testing acidity is optional. You will also need: a measuring cup; an empty quart jar with a lid for mixing ingre-

3: For storing the finished wine you will need: empty, fifth-sized, colored-glass bottles; corks; a corking device (lower left); foil caps; and gummed labels.

1: The basic materials needed for home wine making are: gallon-sized jugs; sugar and measuring cup; rubber cap or cork stopper for an air lock; nylon bag for pressing fruit; plastic air lock shown fitted within a rubber stopper; hydrometer and clear tube for measuring specific gravity; and acid-test strips. In addition you will need a three-gallon-sized plastic bucket and a plastic siphon tube. An assortment of the dry ingredients needed is in the bottom row (from left): sodium metabisulphate in powdered and tablet form; yeast nutrient; wine yeast; and citric acid.

2: If you are making quantities of wine at home, the manual fruit crusher shown at left or a press like the one at right will ease the task of extracting juice from fresh fruit.

dients; sodium metabisulphate tablets; white sugar; wine yeast; wine yeast nutrient in tablet or powdered form; and citric or other acid. For storing the liquid in its primary and secondary fermentation stages, you will need: two empty gallon-sized jugs; clear plastic food wrap or a large sheet of polyethylene; a string or elastic band; a 5-foot plastic siphon tube ⅜ inch thick with a ¼-inch opening; a rubber bung or cork with a hole in the center; and a plastic fermentation lock with cap. To bottle a gallon of wine, you will need: five empty, fifth-sized colored-glass bottles with smooth necks; a corking device; an assortment of No. 8 or No. 9 corks; aluminum-foil cork covers; and blank gummed labels, as shown in photograph 3.

4: Pour metabisulphate solution into any container to be sterilized, such as this primary fermenting bucket of plastic. Wipe the sides of the container with paper towels dipped in the solution.

5: Return the sterilizing solution to its container through a funnel, and seal the container tightly. The sterilizing solution can be used repeatedly for a period of four months before you discard it.

6: Rinse the grapes in cold water; then place them in a sterile primary fermenting bucket. Using your hands or a wooden masher, crush the fruit until all of the skins are split.

7: To separate the juice from the skins and seeds, put the crushed fruit in a nylon bag. Use your hands to squeeze the bag until no more juice can be pressed from the fruit.

Sterilizing a Container

Throughout the wine-making process, you will use a variety of containers for combining ingredients. Sterilize these containers and any other equipment you will use. To prepare the sterilizing solution, dissolve ½ to 1 ounce of sodium metabisulphate in a gallon-sized jar half filled with lukewarm water. This solution is pungent; avoid inhaling it. Pour half of the solution in a container, and wipe the inside with a paper towel dipped in the solution (photograph 4). Then use a funnel to return the solution to the original container (photograph 5). Invert the sterilized container, and shake it well to drain excess moisture. The sterilizing solution can be used repeatedly throughout the wine-making process to disinfect any equipment or container that comes into contact with the wine. If you store the solution in a sealed container, it should remain active for at least four months.

Crushing and Pressing Fruit

Grapes are one of the fruits from which you extract juice by crushing and pressing. Grapes and other fruit for wine making should be at the peak of ripeness, dry on the outside and juicy on the inside. You may need as much as 14 pounds of grapes to make one gallon of wine. Refrigerate the fruit until it is needed.

To make a grape wine, first separate the grape clusters and remove the large stems and leaves which would make the wine bitter. Rinse the grapes well in cold water to minimize the growth of wild yeast or bacteria; they could hinder fermentation. Put half of the grapes in a sterilized bucket, and use your hands, a wooden masher, or a wooden spoon to press down on them (photograph 6). Once the skins split, add the rest of the grapes and crush them the same way. Then hold a nylon or muslin pressing bag over the bucket and scoop the skins, pulp, and seeds of the crushed fruit into the sack. Suspend the sack over the bucket, and twist it to wring out every bit of juice (photograph 7). The fabric bag traps the pulp, pits, stems, and leaves.

To ease the juice-extracting process make a simple pressing device (Figure A, opposite). For this, you will need: two boards approximately 1½ by 4 by 14 inches; a door hinge; wood screws; and a screwdriver. Use the hinge to fasten the boards together at one end. Set the hinged edge of the press on the rim of a bucket and place fruit, in a pressing bag, between the boards. Squeeze the boards closed to extract juice into the bucket.

Dissolve a sodium metabisulphate tablet in eight ounces of the fruit juice for each gallon of finished wine. (Sodium metabisulphate prevents bacteria from forming; as the tablets are premeasured, they are more convenient to use than the powder recommended for cleaning equipment.) Add the tablet solution to the bulk of the juice and stir well. Wait 12 to 24 hours before adding yeast and yeast nutrient.

Controlling Wine Color

Grape wine can be as light in color as the clear juice or as dark as the grape skins. If you prefer a light white wine with a golden sheen, discard the contents of the pressing sack. Then strain the juice into another sterilized bucket, the primary fermenter. If you want a rosé wine with a slight pinkish glint or a red wine rich and robust, place dark grape skins and pulp (but not the seeds) in the bucket of juice. Cover the bucket with clear plastic, secured with string or elastic, to keep out bacteria and dirt. Let the skins bathe in the juice for three to four days for a rosé and about a week for a red wine. Then strain out the pulp and skin as you transfer the juice to another sterilized bucket.

(These general techniques are used to make wine from grapes, but since grapes vary widely in sugar content and acidity, no specific recipe can specify the quantities of grapes, sugar, and acid to use, to produce a particular kind of grape wine.)

Testing for Sugar

During fermentation, yeast converts sugar into alcohol and carbon dioxide. The amount of sugar naturally present in the juice, the strength of the yeast, and the sugar that is added determine the amount of alcohol that will be formed. As a general rule, up to two pounds of sugar may be added for each gallon of wine that is being made.

The best way to regulate the sweetness or dryness of the wine and to obtain consistent results is to use a hydrometer to measure the sugar content (Figure B). By taking a reading of the sugar present in the juice at the outset, you can calculate how much sugar you need to add to raise the sweetness and alcoholic content to suit your taste. Strive for a wine that is slightly dry; sugar can always be added to sweeten a finished wine. (Dry is a term used to describe wine that contains a minimum amount of unfermented sugar.)

To measure the sugar level with a hydrometer, sterilize a plastic or glass tube large enough to hold the hydrometer. (Most wine hydrometers come already packaged in such a plastic tube.) Half-fill the tube with a sample of juice and insert the hydrometer, round end down. The hydrometer will float in the juice. Spin it to eliminate air bubbles that could affect the reading. Hold the vial at eye level. When the liquid settles, take a reading from the hydrometer stem where the surface of the liquid cuts the specific gravity scale. The more sugar in a liquid, the higher the reading will be. To produce a dry wine the specific gravity should register from 1.085 to 1.100 at 60 degrees Fahrenheit; for a medium wine from 1.120 to 1.140, and for a sweet wine from 1.140 to 1.160. The addition of 2¼ ounces of sugar to a gallon of juice will usually raise its specific gravity by 5 degrees (measured as .005 on the specific gravity scale). Using the specific gravity chart provided with a wine hydrometer, you can calculate the amount of sugar to add per gallon to achieve the desired sweetness and alcoholic content.

Adding Sugar

Since undissolved sugar can cause fermentation to slow down too quickly, a sugar syrup should be used to add sugar to the juice. For a more even fermentation, add the sugar in parts, half at first, the remainder during the later stage of secondary fermentation. This produces a drier wine. To begin, bring a quart of juice to a boil in a stainless steel pot and add half the total amount of sugar needed. Let this solution cool before gently stirring it into the juice in the fermenting bucket.

Later you will make a solution with the balance of the sugar by heating it with a pint or more of partially fermented juice. Cool to room temperature; then gently stir this syrup into the rest of the liquid.

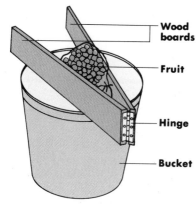

A
Figure A: To crush fruit, you can make a simple press by joining two boards with a hinge. To use the press, rest its edge on the rim of a bucket. Then place fruit, in a pressing bag, between the boards, and close them to squeeze out juice.

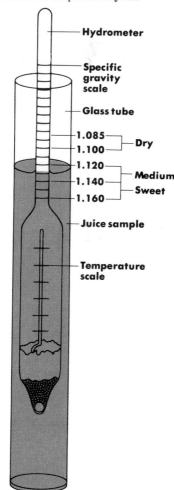

B
Figure B: For sugar testing, set a wine hydrometer in a tube half-to two-thirds filled with a juice sample. Spin the hydrometer to remove air bubbles. Then take a reading where the juice level crosses the hydrometer scale. With the sugar table provided with a wine hydrometer, select the level of wine sweetness that you wish to obtain. Then subtract the present sugar content from the desired one to determine the amount of sugar that you need to add.

8: The liquid being fermented, called must, contains all of the wine-making ingredients. At the stage shown, primary fermentation is complete after one week. Sediment settles slowly so the wine appears hazy.

9: To eliminate sediment, rack the wine by siphoning. Insert a siphon tube in the top of the primary fermentation bucket. Suck on the tube until the wine begins to flow, and insert the free end in a sterile jar. Avoid agitating the bucket during racking so you don't stir up the sediment.

Testing for Acidity

Although acidity will vary with the type of wine you are making, aim for a level between 0.30 and 0.75 percent. Below the lower level, the wine will be dull and insipid. But too high a level of acidity can delay fermentation and give the wine a medicinal taste and unpleasant color. Testing for acidity is an optional step, but one that allows you to adjust the acidity of the juice before fermentation begins.

The simplest way to test acidity is with pH test strips from a wine supply store. When a strip is dipped in a sample of juice, it should become the color that indicates a pH between 3 and 4. Although this gives only a rough estimate of acidity, it is adequate for a beginner. If the juice is not acid enough, you can raise the acidity of each gallon of wine 0.1 percent by gradually adding 1½ teaspoons of citric acid or an acid blend. If the liquid is too acid, you can gradually reduce the acidity 0.10 percent by adding one teaspoon of calcium carbonate or one pint of water for each gallon of wine, until the desired acidity is achieved.

Tannin, an acid present in tea and in the stems and skins of fruit, adds zest to wine and gives it good keeping qualities. You can boost the flavor of flower and grain wines, low in tannin, by adding powdered tannin. Some fruit wines, such as elderberry, may be too high in tannin, requiring that you add small amounts of sugar or glycerine to the finished wine to overcome a harsh taste.

In addition, some fruits such as pears and peaches contain high quantities of pectin which will make the finished wine cloudy. To break down the pectin in these fruits, you can add 1½ grams of pectic enzyme for each gallon of finished wine. (Pectic enzyme is available in powdered and tablet form.)

It's a Must

Once the juice, sodium metabisulphate tablets, any necessary acid or acid neutralizer, and half the sugar are in the primary fermenting bucket, and have been left undisturbed for 12 to 24 hours, you are ready to add the yeast and yeast food, called nutrient, in order to produce must, the unfermented wine. Yeast, a minute living organism, needs sugar, warmth, oxygen, vitamins, and acid to live. For wine making, use one of the special wine yeasts that adds its own flavor to the wine. A good wine yeast will help the wine become stronger and richer in flavor. It also creates a firmer sediment, easing later siphoning and clearing of the wine.

Check to make sure all ingredients in the fermenting bucket are dissolved and are not sticking to the sides of the bucket, and that the liquid is cool. Next, activate wine yeast by adding it to the bucket. Most packets of yeast will ferment five gallons of wine, but you can use a whole packet for one gallon. Also, two yeast nutrient tablets should be added for each gallon of wine juice. Then stir the mixture gently with a wooden spoon until the yeast and nutrient are dissolved. Cover the bucket with plastic wrap held in place with a string. Then set the bucket in a warm place, away from drafts. The ideal temperature for the multiplication of yeast is between 68 and 70 degrees. Stir the must gently every three or four days.

Primary Fermentation

Fermentation starts in the presence of air (photograph 8). As the yeast converts sugar into alcohol, carbon dioxide bubbles are formed. For each bubble that appears on the surface of the must, an equal weight of alcohol has been formed. Primary fermentation will be vigorous at first but may last only three to six days. (With more than one gallon of wine, primary fermentation will last longer.)

Secondary Fermentation

Once the bubbling subsides in the primary fermenting bucket, transfer the wine to an airtight container (photograph 9). Sterilize a gallon-sized jar and a plastic siphon tube with sodium metabisulphate solution. To stabilize and clear the wine, the thick layer of solids that settles in the bottom of the fermenting vessel is removed by siphoning off the wine, a process known as racking. To rack the wine, set the primary fermenting bucket near the edge of your worktable. Handle the bucket very gently to avoid disturbing the sediment, which could impart a bitter taste to the wine. Position the jar on the floor below the bucket. To start the wine flowing, put one end of the plastic tube in the top half of the bucket and suck on the free end of the tube. Once the wine fills half the tube, put the free end into the jar. Push the tube deeper into the bucket as the wine level lowers, but leave the sediment undisturbed (photograph 10). Remove the tube when nearly all the wine is in the jar. Rinse the bucket and tube for the next racking.

Even if you follow the recipe exactly, the jar may not be filled to its rim with wine because you lose a little wine each time you rack. Since bacteria can multiply in the air space, fill the container to its neck with water, canned juice, or sugar syrup. Leave a little space for further bubbling action.

No Admittance

Tiny fruit flies are drawn to fermenting liquid. If one gets into the jar during the second stage of fermentation, bacteria carried by the fly could turn the wine to vinegar. To keep flies and bacteria at bay, seal the fermenting jar with an air lock—preferably a glass or plastic U-shaped tube with two bulbs—fitted into a rubber or cork stopper (photograph 11).

Half-fill the U bend of the air lock with sodium metabisulphate solution, and cap the air lock opening. Next push the lower stem of the air lock into the hole of the stopper. Then push the stopper into the mouth of the jar. If you use a cork stopper, seal the edges around the stopper with melted wax. Set the jar out of direct sunlight where the temperature will be 65 to 70 degrees.

As the wine ferments, the yeast will continue to release carbon dioxide. As the pressure mounts, the gas will push through the solution in the air lock, causing the solution to lodge in one bulb (Figure C). When fermentation slows, rack the wine again. Add the rest of the sugar in solution to replace the sediment left behind. Then allow the jar to stand undisturbed for three or four weeks. When the wine is clear and the sediment is firm, rack the wine into another sterilized gallon-sized jar, the same way you transferred the wine from the primary fermenting bucket. Replace the air lock and stopper. Replace the sterilizing solution once a month to be certain it is still active.

After fermentation has ceased, rack the wine once again. Racking helps stabilize the wine and reduces the risk of after-bottling fermentation (which can burst bottles.) Racking also keeps the wine from acquiring off flavors from dead yeast. When the sodium metabisulphate in the air lock returns to an even level, it usually signals that no more carbon dioxide is being released and fermentation is complete.

Before you bottle the wine, however, double check for gas bubbles that indicate continuing fermentation. This way, you can minimize the possibility of burst bottles. In a white wine, fermentation appears in the form of visible rising gas bubbles. In a red wine, check for bubbles by holding a flashlight against the jar.

Once fermentation has indeed stopped, check the clarity of the wine. But do not be in a hurry to use chemicals or filters to clear it. Rather, let the wine clear naturally in a cool place if it will. If the wine continues to be cloudy, you can filter it during bottling. Or you can add a clearing agent such as isinglass to the wine jar, following package directions.

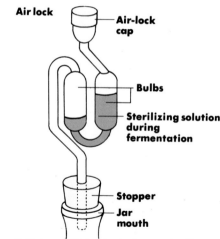

C
Figure C: To insure that no bacteria can enter the wine as it ferments in a gallon jar, seal it with a stopper holding an air lock. Half fill the bulbs of the air lock with sterilizing solution and cap the top. Fit the air lock into the stopper. As the wine ferments, gases are released, forcing the sterilizing solution to lodge in one bulb of the air lock. But when fermentation is finished, the solution in the air lock will return to an even level.

10: If you are careful when you rack the wine, clear wine will be transferred to the jug and the sediment will remain at the bottom of the bucket. To compensate for the loss of sediment that has decreased the volume of the wine, you can fill or top the jar with juice or sugar syrup up to the base of the neck.

11: Seal the jar in which secondary fermentation will take place with a cork or rubber stopper and an air-lock device to keep bacteria and fruit flies out. Press the stopper into the jar mouth. Fill the bulbs of the air lock half full of sterilizing solution, then cap. Put the bottom stem of the air lock into the stopper opening.

12: To use a corker, separate the handles and raise the plunger; then insert a sterilized cork in the middle. Close the handles to compress the cork and center the corker on the bottle. Press down on the plunger to drive the cork into place. The top edge of the cork should be level with the bottle rim.

Bottling, Labeling, and Storing the Wine

Aging, the process of maturing that gives wine a distinctive taste, may take weeks, months, or years in tightly closed bottles. Flat-bottomed, green-colored bottles with smooth necks, each holding one-fifth of a gallon, are ideal for storing wines. Tinted glass keeps light from discoloring wine as it ages. A smooth neck lets you fit a corking device over the mouth of each bottle for easy sealing. (Bottles with concave bottoms are recommended only for champagne and sparkling wines.)

Whether you use new bottles or recycled ones, sterilize them before you fill them with wine. Then invert the bottles to drain them. (Empty beer bottles are fine for sampling the wine at different stages of development.)

Corks are preferred for sealing bottles. To soften the corks for insertion, soak them for half an hour in the sterilizing solution, consisting of ½ of a sodium metabi-sulphate tablet and ½ teaspoon of clear glycerine in a pint of warm water.

To transfer wine from the fermenting jar into a bottle, use the siphoning procedure described on page 2800. Be careful not to agitate any sediment. Fill each bottle within two inches of its rim, and cover the bottle opening with clear plastic wrap. Let the wine stand in the bottles for 24 hours before corking to make sure the siphoning does not restart fermentation. As long as the wine has an alcoholic content of at least 10 percent, it will not be affected by vinegar-causing bacteria.

Although there are other tools for hammering a cork into a bottle, the easiest way to obtan a tight seal is with an inexpensive metal corker (photograph 12). To operate, you separate the handles and put a cork in the center. Then you squeeze the handles to compress the cork. Next, center the corker over the mouth of the bottle and bear down on the plunger with a firm, even pressure.

To record the bottling date and the type of wine, fasten a gummed label inscribed with the pertinent information just below the bottle's shoulder. If the wine is to your liking, you will want to make another batch the same way.

There are several ways to arrange storage space that will provide the temperature required. Bottled wine should be kept in a cool, dim place. The temperatures should be fairly constant, about 60 degrees Fahrenheit. A wine bottle should be stored on its side so the cork stays wet and tight but allows the wine to breathe. If you live in a house, the basement usually offers the best storage area, away from the furnace and dryer. But if you live in an apartment, a closet or the space under a bed will do. To make the most of a small space, you can stack bottles in a pyramid shape. Or you can store bottles, stacked sideways, in empty wine cartons with cardboard dividers from a liquor store. The dividers keep the bottles from rolling against each other, lessening the risk of breakage. Such cartons will also serve to contain flying fragments of glass in the event that a bottle bursts, although that possibility can be minimized if you make sure fermentation has ended before you seal the bottle (page 2801).

Although the alcoholic content of wine is at its height when it is bottled, the longer the wine is allowed to age undisturbed, the mellower it will become. A wine made from a vegetable usually takes longer to mature than one made from fruit.

Selecting and Serving Wine

When you choose a wine, let taste be your guide. Some prefer a hearty, robust red wine with such foods as red meat, and a white wine with fish or fowl, but there is no firm rule about this. However, dry or medium wines are a better complement for main dishes, while sweet wines are more suitable with desserts. If a wine is too dry, you can always sweeten it by adding sugar. There is not much you can do with a wine that is too sweet except blend it with a similar wine that is too dry.

Set a bottle of red wine upright four to 24 hours before serving to allow sediment to settle. Uncork the bottle an hour or two before serving to let the wine breathe and to release any acid smell and taste. Chill a bottle of white wine for half an hour in an ice bucket, or place it in a refrigerator four hours before serving.

A wine glass should contain six or seven ounces of wine. Choose one with a tulip-shaped bowl, curving slightly inward at its rim to hold the wine's fragrance. The bowl should display the wine's color. A stem enables you to hold the glass comfortably while the wine stays cool. When serving, fill the wine glass half full.

For related entries, see "Brewing," "Herbs," "Marmalades and Preserves," "Organic Gardening," and "Vinegars."

A WINE FOR ANYTIME

To make a white wine, grape skins and pulp are removed from the juice immediately after pressing. But for a dark wine, the skin and pulp are left to soak in the juice until the desired color is achieved.

The calendar of homemade wine on the pages that follow offers 12 folk-wine recipes, one for each month of the year. With these recipes, each yielding one gallon of wine, you can experiment with such exotic wine-making ingredients as rose petals, apples, rice, even pea pods.

JANUARY
Raisin wine

1¾ pounds minced large raisins
1¾ pounds sugar
1 teaspoon citric acid
1 sodium metabisulphate tablet
Montrachet (an all-purpose wine yeast), Sauterne, or Chablis wine yeast
Yeast nutrient

Boil the raisins in water for 1 hour. Then put half of the total amount of sugar in a fermenting bucket. Strain the raisin juice over the sugar and stir well. Once the juice cools to room temperature, add the sterilizing tablet and citric acid. Wait at least 12 hours before adding yeast and nutrient, and stir the must. (All-purpose yeast will begin to ferment within 24 to 48 hours.) Set the covered bucket in a warm place about 1 week. Then siphon the wine into a jar and top it with sugar syrup. Seal the jar with an air lock. As the wine clears, rack again, adding sugar syrup. When fermentation ceases, rack the wine into bottles and cork. Age raisin wine at least 1 year before opening.

FEBRUARY
Elderberry or blueberry wine

¼ pound dried elderberries or blueberries
4 ounces chopped raisins (optional)
2 pounds sugar
1 gallon water
1 teaspoon citric acid
1 sodium metabisulphate tablet
Bordeaux or Montrachet wine yeast
Yeast nutrient

Combine the berries and raisins with 1 pound of sugar in a fermenting bucket. Pour boiling water over the fruit and stir well. When the liquid cools add the sodium metabisulphate and citric acid. Wait 12 hours and add the yeast and nutrient, and stir again. Set the bucket in a warm place for 1 week and cover. Stir daily, pushing the fruit down for the first 3 or 4 days. After 1 week strain the must into another bucket, and rack the wine into a fermenting jar. When fermentation slows, add the rest of the sugar syrup and stir well. Rack the wine several times until it is clear and fermentation is complete, then bottle. Age an elderberry wine for 1 year and a blueberry wine 6 months to a year.

MARCH
Rice wine (sake)

3 pounds of rice
1 pound chopped raisins
2¼ pounds sugar
1 gallon warm water
2 tablespoons citric acid
1 sodium metabisulphate tablet
Pinch of isinglass
Sherry wine yeast or Montrachet wine yeast
Yeast nutrient

Put the rice, raisins, and half the sugar in a fermenting bucket, and soak in the warm water. When the water reaches room temperature, sterilize the juice with a sodium metabisulphate tablet. Twelve hours later, add the dissolved yeast, yeast nutrient, and citric acid; then sprinkle in a pinch of isinglass. Loosely cover the bucket. Stir often the first 3 days; then leave the bucket undisturbed in a warm place for 6 more days. Strain the must, siphon into a closed fermenting jar, and seal it with an air lock. When fermentation slows, add the rest of the sugar syrup. Allow the wine to clear naturally. When fermentation is complete and the wine clear, bottle the wine. This young wine is harsh, but it improves with age.

APRIL
Dandelion wine

2 quarts fresh dandelion heads
Peels of 4 oranges
2½ pounds sugar
1 gallon boiling water
1 sodium metabisulphate tablet
Montrachet wine yeast and yeast nutrient

Gather dandelions at the end of April or the beginning of May on a sunny day when the flowers are completely open and dry. Pick only the heads, no stems or green at all. Place the flower heads in a fermenting bucket, and cover them with the boiling water. Steep the flowers for 2 days in the loosely covered bucket and stir daily. (Do not let the flowers steep more than 48 hours or the wine will acquire a bad odor.) Then pour the flowers and water into a large saucepan, add the orange peels (no white pith), and boil for 10 minutes. Put half the sugar in the bucket; strain the flower and peel juice onto it and stir the liquid. When the liquid cools, add a sterilizing tablet. Twelve hours later add the yeast and nutrient and stir well. Ferment the must for 1 week; siphon it into a jar and seal with an air lock. Rack the wine and add sugar syrup. Bottle when fermentation ends. Wait 8 months to a year before drinking.

MAY
Mead or honey wine

4 pounds honey
Juice of 1 orange
Juice of 1 lemon
1 gallon water
1 sodium metabisulphate tablet
Mead wine yeast or Montrachet wine yeast
Yeast nutrient
Pectic enzyme

For this recipe, it is important to use a good nutrient, since honey does not naturally have the necessary minerals. Otherwise, the procedure is standard. Bring the water and honey to the boil, and let it cool. Add the fruit juice and sterilizing tablet. Twelve hours later introduce the pectic enzyme, yeast, and nutrient. Ferment the must in a covered bucket for 4 to 7 days or until the vigorous fermentation dies down. Then siphon the wine into a closed jug fitted with an air lock. Rack the wine when necessary until fermentation stops. (Fermentation may take a bit longer than for most wines.) Then bottle the wine and allow it to age for at least 1 year.

JUNE
Rose petal wine

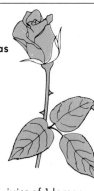

4 pints rose petals (as fragrant as possible)
2 pounds sugar
1 lemon
1 gallon water
1 sodium metabisulphate tablet
Montrachet wine yeast
Yeast nutrient

Place the rose petals, juice of 1 lemon, and 1 pound of the sugar in the fermenting bucket and cover with 1 gallon boiling water. When the liquid cools to 70 degrees Fahrenheit, add the sterilizing tablet. Wait at least 12 hours before adding the yeast and nutrient. Cover the bucket and set in a warm place for a week, stirring daily. Then strain the must into another container. (If a lighter-colored wine is desired, remove the rose petals from the must a few days earlier.) Siphon the wine into a fermenting jar and seal with an air lock. When the fermentation slows down, add the rest of the sugar in solution. Ferment, rack, and bottle the wine as usual. Age one year.

JULY

Raspberry wine

3½ pounds rasp-
  berries
2 to 2½ pounds sugar
1 gallon water
1 sodium metabi-
  sulphate tablet
Montrachet or
  Burgundy wine
  yeast
Yeast nutrient

Place the raspberries and 1¼ pounds of sugar in a primary fermenting bucket and cover with boiling water. When the water cools to room temperature, crush the fruit with clean hands or a press, and add the sterilizing tablet. At least 12 hours later it is safe to add the yeast and nutrient. Stir well. Cover and keep the must in a warm, draft-free spot. Once the froth subsides, about 3 to 4 days, run the wine through a nylon sack or a colander to remove the pulp. Then siphon the must into a jar and attach an air lock. Add the remainder of sugar syrup when fermentation slows. When a sediment layer forms, siphon the wine off and replace the air lock. When the wine stops fermenting, siphon once more and bottle the wine. Allow the wine to age for a year.

AUGUST

Pea pod wine

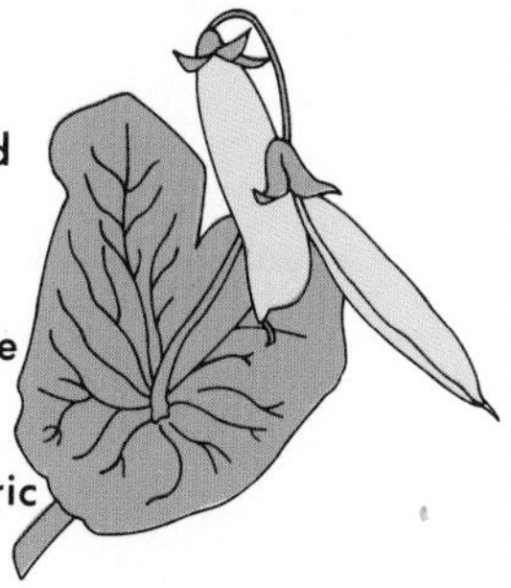

4 pounds shucked
  pea pods
2¼ pounds
  sugar
½ teaspoon grape
  tannin
1 gallon water
2 tablespoons citric
  acid
1 sodium metabi-
  sulphate tablet
Montrachet wine yeast
Yeast nutrient

Wash the pea pods and boil them in water until they are tender. Put 1⅛ pounds of sugar in a fermenting bucket and dissolve with the strained pea pod juice. When the liquid cools add the sodium metabisulphate tablet. Wait at least 12 hours before adding the tannin, yeast, nutrient, and citric acid. Let the must stand for 1 week in the loosely sealed bucket and stir daily. Then rack the wine into a gallon-sized jar and plug with an air lock. Add sugar syrup when the fermentation slows. As the wine begins to clear, rack again. Bottle when fermentation is complete. Age for one year.

SEPTEMBER

Apple wine

5 pounds Macintosh
  apples
Pectic enzyme
2¼ pounds sugar
1 lemon
1 gallon water
½ pound chopped
  raisins
1 sodium metabi-
  sulphate tablet
Chablis wine yeast
Yeast nutrient

Wash and cut the apples, skins and all, into small chunks. Place the apples in a saucepan, and simmer in water for 20 minutes until soft. Put 1⅛ pounds of sugar in a fermenting bucket. Then strain liquid from the apples, pouring it over the sugar. Stir well. When the juice is cool, add the sodium metabisulphate. Wait 12 hours and add the yeast, nutrient, pectic enzyme, and lemon juice. Then cover the bucket loosely and set it in a warm place for 4 to 7 days. Rack the wine into a gallon-sized jar and insert an air lock. Add sugar syrup as necessary when fermentation slows. After 1 month rack the wine again and add the raisins to the brew. Keep the wine under air lock for 6 months before straining and bottling. Then age the wine for 6 months to a year.

OCTOBER

Pear wine

4 pounds ripe pears
Citric acid
2¼ pounds sugar
Pectic enzyme
1 gallon water
1 sodium metabi-
  sulphate tablet
Montrachet wine
  yeast
Yeast nutrient

Chop the whole pears into small bits, saving the juice, and place them in a saucepan filled with the water. When the water boils, turn down and simmer the fruit for 20 minutes. Next, place 1⅛ pounds of sugar in a fermenting bucket and strain the pear juice and juice saved from chopping the pears into the bucket. Stir gently until the sugar dissolves. When the juice reaches room temperature, sterilize it with sodium metabisulphate. Then wait at least 12 hours before adding the pectic enzyme, yeast, and nutrient. Let the must stand in a loosely sealed container for 1 week. Then rack the wine into a fermenting jar and close with an air lock. Add sugar syrup when fermentation slows. Bottle the wine when fermentation is complete. Age one year.

NOVEMBER

Celery wine

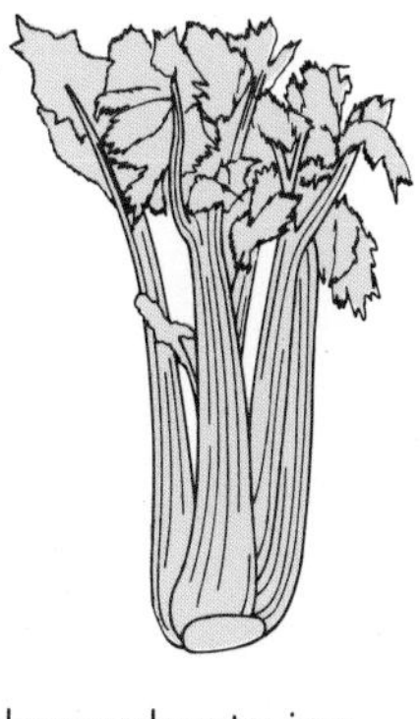

3 pounds chopped
  green celery
2¼ pounds brown
  sugar or honey
2 tablespoons citric
  acid
1 gallon water
1 sodium metabi-
  sulphate tablet
Montrachet wine
  yeast
Yeast nutrient

Place the chopped celery and water in a pot, and bring to the boil until it is tender. Put 1⅛ pounds of sugar in the fermenting bucket and strain the celery juice into the bucket, stirring until the sugar dissolves. Once the juice cools to about 70 degrees, add the sodium metabisulphate. At least 12 hours later add the citric acid, yeast, and nutrient, and stir well. Cover the bucket and set it in a warm place for 4 days. Then rack the wine into a fermenting jar and seal with an air lock. As fermentation slows, add the remaining sugar syrup. When fermentation is complete, bottle the wine. Celery wine is slightly bitter and makes a fine apéritif. Allow to age for one year.

DECEMBER

Beetroot wine

2¼ pounds beets,
  preferably small
5 cloves
1 ounce bruised
  ginger
2¼ pounds
  sugar
Juice of 1 lemon
1 gallon water
1 sodium metabi-
  sulphate tablet
Montrachet wine yeast
Yeast nutrient

Wash the beets, cut them up, and boil them until tender. Put the cloves, ginger, and 1⅛ pounds of sugar in a bucket. Strain the beet juice over the dry ingredients. When the liquid cools add the sodium metabisulphate tablet and lemon juice. Twelve hours later, add the yeast and nutrient and stir well. Cover the bucket and put it in a warm spot for 3 days. Then strain the must into another bucket, and siphon it into a gallon-sized jar. Seal the jar with an air lock. When fermentation slows, add the remainder of the sugar syrup. As the wine clears, rack it again before bottling. Allow to age for one year.

WINTER SCULPTURE
Playing It Cool

The annals of art history do not record who built the first snowman. Though children have been sculpting with snow for a long time, it was not until the 1920s that the artistic possibilities of the transitory medium were exploited in the United States. At that time, students at Dartmouth College in New Hampshire, tiring of simple snowmen, began to try more ambitious snow sculptures. They found they could control the snow better if they wet it down to form a workable slush. In the spirit of competition, other Dartmouth students were soon at work on more ambitious projects, and before long Dartmouth's winter carnival became one of the most famous college events in the nation. Its lead was quickly followed by many other colleges in snow country. Eventually the idea moved off the campuses and into towns and cities across the northern United States and Canada. Huge snow sculptures became annual community projects. Today, many families create quite elaborate snow sculptures in their own yards.

Jim Haskins is the author of Snow Sculpture and Ice Carving *(Macmillan, Inc.). In addition to writing 24 books, he is a teacher, consultant, reviewer, and a snow-sculpture enthusiast.*

Outdoor Activities
Snow sculptures   ¢ ▣ 👫 🎇

Building even a basic snowman will give you a feeling of accomplishment, and in the process you will learn quite a bit about snow as a sculpture medium. The more you understand it, the more control you will have. Snow can have a variety of consistencies, ranging from dry and powdery (when the temperature is below 25 degrees Fahrenheit) to downright sloppy (when the temperature gets much above freezing). The ideal consistency for snow sculpture is on the slushy side, as on a warm day after a heavy snowfall. But if only powdery snow is available, it can be made workable by mixing it with small amounts of water. A way to do this is described on page 2808.

With any snow consistency, some trial-and-error is necessary to learn how the weight of the snow will affect the sculpting process. Many a sculpture-in-the-making has toppled because the center of gravity was in the wrong place. With practice, you will gain a feeling for balancing weight with the snow's cohesiveness.

There is one property of snow beyond your control. When the sun shines upon it, or the temperature rises, it will melt.

Planning
Even a simple snow sculpture requires planning so it can be displayed to good advantage. Monumental campus structures and community projects, such as the one shown at right, are often planned well in advance of the first snowfall.

To begin, consider the space in which you will build. If your yard is small, the sculpture should be of a similar scale. Try to make it interesting from any viewpoint. Consider the background, especially if you will not color your sculpture or spotlight it with colored lights (page 2811). A white sculpture benefits from a dark background—a clump of evergreens, a brick wall, a fence painted a dark color. Consider also the height and the amount of heavy lifting required.

Draw your sculpture on paper, preferably to scale. When you work with snow, you will find your eye is not a very reliable measuring device. Even if you adopt a design from a picture, it is a good idea to make scale drawings.

Tools and Methods
Your hands are the best tools available, for snow can be shaped better with hands than with any other tool. At the start, wear heavy, waterproof gloves, but when

This monumental snow jester enlivens a plaza in Quebec City, Canada. Named *Bonhomme Carnaval*, it is 20 feet tall.

A snow sphinx gazes enigmatically across the barren wastes of suburbia. Though not as ambitious or enduring as the well-known Egyptian sphinx, making it was great fun for three snow sculptors. How it was built is described on page 2811.

you come to fine details, work with bare hands for short periods, if you can stand the cold. In addition to improving control, bare hands produce the right amount of heat to make snow easy to sculpt. When you work with slush, once the slush has frozen, you need a small hatchet for carving and a hammer and wide chisel for smoothing the surface.

Using slush, you become more involved in carving than in packing. Once the basic form is frozen, carve rough outlines with the hatchet. Keep the center of gravity low, and provide plenty of support for weighty parts. As you begin to carve details, switch to the chisel for more delicate operations. Control is important, but if you make a mistake, you can plaster more slush on the damaged area, let it freeze, and begin anew. A fine spray of water applied to the finished carving will help smooth the rough places and strengthen the details.

Some sculptors of hard-packed snow spray the entire finished work with water to give it a coat of ice. This gives the work a good appearance, but the ice does not reflect the sun as well as white snow, so the sculpture absorbs more heat and, accordingly, melts sooner.

A Slush-Bucket System

An assembly line for making slush can be set up with two or three household buckets. The larger the containers, the better. Keep hot water in the first container, replenishing it from time to time as it cools or is used up. Fill the second container with snow, adding small quantities of hot water from the first bucket to melt it. From the second container pour a little cool water into the third, and add enough snow to form a slushy mixture. When a consistency suitable for making hard-packed snowballs is reached, the mixture is right for sculpture. Using hot water

The annual winter carnival at Sapporo, Japan, is an exciting forum for the display of snow and ice sculptures. When the 1972 Winter Olympics were also held there, this huge sculpture was among the many built to commemorate the games. It depicts Kintaro, the legendary Japanese baby and athlete par excellence who mastered the beasts of the forest with his physical prowess. In this updated rendition, Kintaro carries the Olympic torch, and a pun on his name, which means "Golden Boy," is incorporated in the gold medal on his chest.

Winter carnival arrives and a residential street in Quebec is transformed. Lined with snow sculptures, it has become a temporary art gallery.

and an extra bucket to melt snow saves time, for a little hot water will go a long way, but you can simplify the process by using cold water and only two buckets.

For large projects, an interior support called an armature is usually necessary. Most of the Dartmouth Winter Carnival sculptures, such as a 38-foot statue (built in 1939) of the founder of the college, would not be possible without armature support. In fact, two armatures are made, one a scale model and the other full-sized. The model is used to study weight and balance, to learn what will work and what will not. This lets the students find out where the problems lie while they are working with pounds rather than tons of snow.

Armatures

Armatures are especially useful if a design involves protruding parts, such as extended arms that would collapse if they were not reinforced. Some snow-sculpture purists avoid secondary materials. There are practical reasons for doing this, for wood and wire conduct heat into the figure and shorten its life. Figure A shows a typical armature and the finished sculpture it supports. But there have been many successful 10-foot-tall sculptures without a bit of wood or wire in them.

When working on a large scale, whether you use an armature or not, always consider the hazards of a collapsing sculpture. A single cubic yard of hard-packed, icy snow weighs up to three-quarters of a ton; the danger it poses is not to be taken lightly. For safety's sake, never allow small children to try to topple a large sculpture.

Be sure to record your sculpture with a camera, for it may last only a few days. It is best to photograph snow sculptures when the sun is shining across them, producing shadows that make details stand out clearly.

An appropriate subject for a snow tableau is this Eskimo dogsledder atop a snow hill on Carnaval Street, Quebec. The sculpted figures are arranged to accommodate an archway leading to an alley between houses.

A

Figure A: An armature made of electrical cable and scrap wood wired or nailed together is an internal structure for supporting the weight of snow that would otherwise collapse. The armature should rest near the bottom of the areas it will support, rather than in the middle, and all bridging segments should be connected to a firm foundation, such as this lion's foreleg or rump.

1: The simplest way to move quantities of snow to the sculpture site is to build up snow boulders by rolling hard-packed snowballs along the ground.

2: Approximate the shape of the finished sculpture (in this case, the sphinx) by arranging the boulders in tiers. A six-three-one progression, shown here as it nears completion, is one of many possibilities. Limit the sculpture to your own height or you will exhaust yourself on the preliminaries.

3: The final pile of snow boulders, stacked in three layers, already suggests the rough outline of the sphinx head, shoulders, and chest. Pack snow under the bottom boulders for stability.

4: With loose snow, fill in all gaps to form a continuous mass. You can remove excess snow with a chopping motion of the hand. If the snow gets icy, a hatchet is needed for this step.

5: Once the basic outline is completed, add snow as necessary for details and appendages, and refine the shape to merge with them as you work. Here the sphinx beard and chest begin to take form.

Coloring and Lighting

Most people prefer snow to be its natural color, but coloring, used carefully, can create striking effects. A snow butterfly, for example, can be colored with a rainbow of vegetable dyes. Or a white snow church can be given multicolored stained-glass windows. It is difficult to lighten colors once they are applied, but it is easy to darken them. Experiment on a small square of hard-packed snow before you apply color to your sculpture. Use an eye-dropper for small areas, a laundry atomizer for larger spaces.

Colored lighting is sometimes used on untinted sculptures. Try combinations like a blue or green light directed at the front of a sculpture and a yellow or red light directed at the back. A turreted snow castle will acquire dimension when lighted from behind with blue and will sparkle when front-lit with yellow or orange.

A Snow Sphinx

Anyone who can build a snowman is on the way to being a snow sculptor, as this first project shows. At first, limit yourself to a compact form, one that can be made by stacking a number of snow boulders into a solid, bottom-heavy shape. For example, the sphinx shown on page 2806 has a low, self-contained mass. It was built on a warm morning, several days after a heavy snowfall, when the snow consistency was perfect. Wet snow is heavy, though, and you may be surprised by how tired you will be after making ten boulders and lifting three or four of them a few feet off the ground.

Preparing the Basic Shape

Begin your sculpture by drawing the form you want to make and calculating the number and size of the snow boulders needed to rough out its basic shape. For the sphinx, you need a bottom layer of six boulders, each about 18 inches in diameter, set in two rows of three; a second layer of three similar boulders; and a single boulder on top for the head. Form the boulders as you would in making a snowman, starting with a small, well-packed snowball and rolling it around to gather more and more snow (photograph 1). You can save work if you can arrange to arrive at the sculpture site just as the boulder reaches the right size. The boulders are assembled in tiers (photograph 2). The finished rough form is shown in photograph 3. To stabilize the top boulder, pack extra snow around its base.

Filling In

Using loose handfuls of snow, fill in the spaces between the boulders so the sculpture becomes one continuous mass of snow. Then hack away any unwanted portions of the original boulders (photograph 4). Work first around the bottom, where the snow is weakest, underpinning and supporting the base layer. Then consult your drawing so you can begin to form the gross outlines of major details. The snow that eventually will form the sphinx's beard is now added (photograph 5). Then the rough outlines of flowing hair and pawlike arms are made (photograph 6). Don't worry about details at this stage.

Details

The finishing touches, as in any sculpture, require the most care. Facial expressions, for example, are often frustrating in snow because they tend to look like caricatures. Each sculpture poses different problems. You may find the mysterious visage of a sphinx is hard to capture; the ears will tend to be grotesque, the shape of the head chunky, the eyes won't focus, the mouth will smirk and pout (photograph 7). It is necessary to add and subtract snow carefully, constantly referring to the drawing. Eventually, gloves may seem unwieldy. In addition to allowing more control, bare hands give off warmth which makes the snow easier to mold. In time the sphinx's face will take shape. Pennies placed in the eyes and partly covered with snow help to focus the gaze; a twig inserted between the lips will give definition to the mouth. Next, make shallow grooves in the hair and on the breastplate. Such low-relief details add textural interest to the shiny, white mass (photograph 8). If you intend to take pictures, deepen and exaggerate all lines as a finishing touch, and clear the surrounding area of accumulated snow debris. The best time to photograph snow sculptures is when the sun shines at right angles to the camera.

6: With most of the parts roughed out, including hair and arms, the more exacting work of refining details can begin. The head is flattened, the shoulders rounded, and the ears added.

7: By trial and error, the head, torso, and arms take definite shape. Bare hands work best in shaping facial details.

8: The finished sculpture includes deep grooves to make the parts stand out from each other. Such exaggeration is often necessary to improve the visual effect.

This snow sculpture of an elephant, weighing tons, required the support of an interior armature.

This ice lion was carved by a professional chef for a banquet at a New York hotel.

Carving and Molding
Ice sculptures

Ice carving differs in many ways from snow sculpture. Unlike snow, which can be built up or carved away, block ice can only be chipped off like marble. It is difficult to carve, for it cracks and splits easily. But for those who work with it, the artistic possibilities of ice are greater than those of snow. For more than a century, chefs in northern Europe have used ice carvings decoratively at banquets, and in America ice carving is part of the curriculum for student chefs. A decorative ice display makes a table look elegant and sumptuous.

Refrigeration has made ice carving possible for the layman, as well as making it easier for the professional. While ice carving is still primarily associated with lavish dining, countless outdoor and indoor projects are done just for fun. Ice carving, particularly on a small scale, can be an individual undertaking, but there are possibilities for large group projects, such as the ice palace shown on page 2816.

Every sculptural medium has its own peculiar properties and ice is no exception. As you work with it, you transform not only its shape but its color and texture. Each carving mark will reflect a different color. The translucency of ice is a unique characteristic. Its color changes as the light changes. Indoors or out, it can be a light show, and the better the ice, the more light it will reflect.

If you are planning an ice sculpture, it is likely that you will obtain your ice from an ice dealer. Artificial ice contains no foreign matter, but it poses other problems.

Artificial ice is often milky looking. It photographs well, but it isn't as easy to carve as natural ice. Artificial ice becomes brittle in a warm room, and it seems to break at the worst possible moment. To minimize such breakage, carve in a cool place, preferably in an unheated outdoor shed.

You can order ice in a variety of sizes, but a 50-pound block is the smallest a beginner should try. It will be delivered as a rough block. Before you begin to carve, smooth all sides. Square each face with a T square and ruler; then cut off gross irregularities with any handsaw.

All ice is somewhat fragile; so carve with care. Never try to chip off big chunks with a chisel; you are likely to crack the entire block. From the beginning, chip away tiny fragments. Handle the ice as little as possible; body heat speeds melting.

Butting rams seem well-matched opponents in this nearly symmetrical ice sculpture.

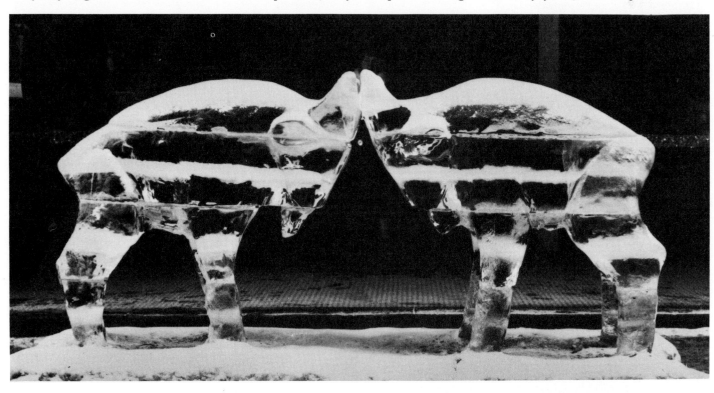

As with chipping any hard material, sharp flying fragments are a safety hazard; so wear sculptors' safety goggles.

If you work outdoors with no enclosure, carve during the morning or late afternoon when the sun is not high. Keep the ice block in shade, out of direct sunshine, even if the temperature is below freezing.

The Sculpting Process

Plan your ice sculpture in detail. Consider how and where you will display it. It is unlikely that you will carve where you will display your sculpture; so plan how you will move it. It will be lighter than the original block, but it will also be more fragile. If it is to be displayed outdoors, make sure the spot where it is placed is level. Place it as high as possible to maximize light reflection and visibility. An oblong slab of ice standing on end is a good display stand, as is a table covered with snow or pine boughs.

To make the swan pictured below, right, or any similar sculpture, the only tools you need are two chisels—one V shaped, the other flat—a ruler, T square, and saw.

Work out the design on paper with drawings the same size you intend your sculpture to be. Make drawings for each of the sides and for the top (Figure B). These drawings should be accurate, and each should contain an outline of the block. If you find the sculpture hard to visualize, make a clay model first, and work out the drawings by viewing the model from five sides. Or use Figure B as a pattern. On the drawings, mark sections of ice to be cut away. Start with a relatively simple subject, and tackle more intricate designs later.

Transfer your drawings to the surfaces of the ice, using the grooved chisel to outline all five faces. Begin chiseling well outside the outline, allowing space for error.

2814   Ice angels linked in a heart shape are a decoration for a wedding party.   A swan of carved ice makes an attractive centerpiece for a buffet table.

Use the V-shaped chisel to do all the initial cutting. When you arrive at the rough form, change to the flat chisel. If you are right-handed, start on the left side of the front and work your way across to the right. (Do the opposite if you are left-handed.) Turn the corner to the right side of the sculpture, complete the carving there, and work your way around. Stand back frequently to make sure the sculpture isn't lopsided. Compare the top of the sculpture with your drawing. It is here that incipient errors are easiest to catch. In any area, make the final pass of the chisel with dispatch so the heat of your hands does not work against you.

Decorative Ice Blocks

Ice can be used decoratively in other ways. Interesting ice cubes can be made, for example, by freezing cherries, olives, or pieces of lemon inside.

For freezing objects in ice on a larger scale, the two methods are molding and implanting. For the first, choose the mold and decide what you want to freeze in it. Household buckets make good molds if the objects are of an appropriate size. Try holly and berries at Christmas, pine cones or leaves in the fall, pussy willows or flowers in the spring. Suspend the object inside the mold with a fine wire; then fill the mold about nine-tenths of the way to the top with water (water expands as it freezes). When the water is sufficiently frozen to hold the object in place, pull out the wire and leave the object in the middle of the block.

The second method involves carving space in the middle of the block for the object to be inserted. Once it is in place, pour water in until it is level with the top of the block. Then freeze it.

For related projects and crafts, see "Carving," "Ice Cream, Sherbet, and Ices," "Molding Methods," "Sand Characters and Castles," and "Sculpture."

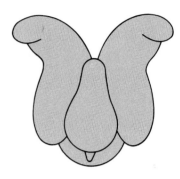

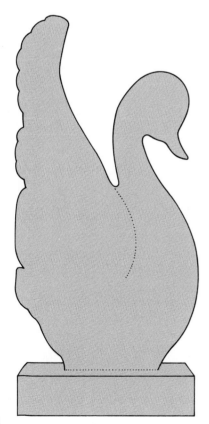
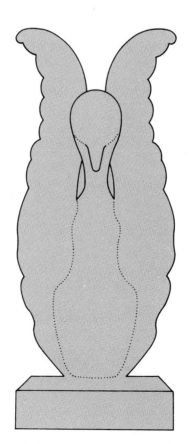
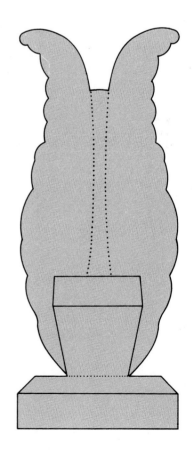

B

Figure B: Ice sculpting is simplified by the use of patterns worked out in advance on paper, one for each side and one for the top. These pattern lines should be scribed on the surfaces of the block. In a symmetrical sculpture such as the swan pictured opposite, the right and left sides (above left) are mirror images of each other. The outlines of the front and back (above, center and right) include dotted lines to indicate major surface changes, as the start of the wings. The top view (upper right) is the most useful view of all in forestalling error, since from it all four sides can be envisioned at once.

Nature made the snow sculpture above, complete with turreted castles and weird beasts, in a single night. But thousands of man-hours of labor went into the structure below, a large, intricately carved, and beautifully lit ice castle in the city of Quebec.